TOTAL
PRESENCE

Thomas J. J. Altizer

TOTAL PRESENCE

The Language of Jesus
and
The Language of Today

THE SEABURY PRESS, NEW YORK

1980
The Seabury Press
815 Second Avenue
New York, N.Y. 10017

Printed in the United States of America

Library of Congress Cataloging in Publication Data
Altizer, Thomas J J
Total presence.

1. History (Theology) 2. Jesus Christ — Parables.
3. Christianity and language. 4. Kingdom of God.
5. Eschatology. I. Title.
BR115.H5A43   230   80-16834   ISBN 0-8164-0461-5

For Ray L. Hart

CONTENTS

Chapter One

THE PARABOLIC JESUS

THE THEOLOGICAL PROBLEM OF SPEECH

Nothing is more distinctive of the biblical tradition or traditions than the centrality therein of Word or speech. Whether in its enactment of Creation, of Covenant, of Torah, of Messiah, of Wisdom, or of Kingdom of God, we may observe here the primacy of speech, and not simply the primacy of speech but also the ultimacy or finality of speech. Nothing truly parallel to this ultimacy and centrality of speech may be found in other mythical and religious traditions, except for its prefigurations in the ancient Near East and its later expressions in Judaism, Christianity, and Islam. India and China embody reverse parallels to this primacy of speech, for here silence and emptiness effect and express a comparable primacy and finality. While speech cannot be said to be primal or ultimate in the Greek religious and mythical traditions as such, it is so in the Homeric epics and in Greek tragedy, and the historical coming together of

1

classical culture and the Bible in Christendom can give us a decisive clue to the unique identity and role of literature in the Western tradition. Nothing comparable to Dante, Milton, or Blake may be found in non-Western literary traditions, for nowhere else is God, the sacred, or the ultimate fully spoken, nowhere else is it truly realized or actualized in language itself. Here God is not simply the object of speech, but the subject of speech as well, as subject which the Christian identifies as the Word of revelation.

Ultimate or final Word speaks in the Bible, and this is a unique historical phenomenon, with the exception of the Koran. A distinctively Christian hermeneutics has good reason to identify the prophetic oracle as the originating center of the Bible, a center which is reenacted in the eschatological proclamation of the New Testament. But neither eschatological proclamation nor prophetic oracle can be understood so long as the theological identity of speech remains unveiled. We know that the speaker of "I" of the prophetic oracle is Yahweh or the Lord, just as we know that the speaker of eschatological proclamation is Spirit, or Son of Man, or one who speaks under the impact of the dawning or near advent of Kingdom of God. But we have not taken with sufficient seriousness the theological consequences of such an identity. Speech here is divine speech or Word of God, or known in faith to be Word of God. Hence the God of faith is not only a revealed God, but also a revealing God, a "speaking" God, and Christianity can only be a reversal of its original ground if it comes to know a God who is ultimately silent.

Christianity and Christianity alone knows a Word or speech which is the absolute antithesis of silence. Here, Word

speaks finally or eschatologically, and Word speaks finally
because Word irreversibly becomes "flesh." Nowhere in the
New Testament is the finality of speech more evident than in
the language of Jesus as recorded in the synoptic Gospels. Of
course, there are many forms of this language in the Gospels,
and these reflect various and conflicting ecclesiastical traditions. But there is virtually unanimous scholarly agreement
that the parabolic language of the Gospels is closest to the
original language of Jesus. While there is a variety of parables
in the Gospels, and some may not have their source in Jesus,
there is common critical agreement that it is in those parables
unique to Jesus that we are given our clearest way of access to
the original Jesus. True, there are good reasons to believe
that none of the Gospel parables contain more than fragments of the actual language of Jesus. But even if only fragments, they are fragments of incredible power, and in some
decisive sense they make manifest and hearable the revolutionary presence and future of the Kingdom of God. Indeed,
here the presence and future of the Kingdom of God tend to
coalesce and become one, and so much so that nonparabolic
language breaks down in attempting to express a parabolic
meaning of time.

Parable is a rare literary genre, if it is a literary genre at all,
and it can initially best be understood by contrasting it with
all other forms or genres of literature. It is not simply a story,
or not simply like other stories, and it has no meaning which
is independent of itself. Moreover, the true parable has no
"author," or no author who is manifest in the parable, and
this because a fully parabolic language gives no sign of either
a source or a purpose lying outside of itself. Perhaps we could
say that the intention of parable is to realize an enactment of

speech wherein a totality of speakable or realizable identity is wholly present and immediately at hand. Therein parable is the antithesis of allegory, and the antithesis of allegory because in its full expression it leaves behind all simile and metaphor. Not until the twentieth century, with the advent of a literature of antimetaphor or purely negative metaphor, did this meaning of the New Testament parable become manifest. For the pure parable so centers the attention of its hearer upon its enactment as to end all awareness of a meaning or an identity beyond its immediate arena of speech.

In this sense parable, or pure parable, is present only in its enactment, only in its telling or saying. Therefore, it can pass into writing only with a loss of its original immediacy, a loss which occasions a reversal of itself, a reversal effecting its fall into the language of simile and metaphor, a fall culminating in its full reversal in allegory. Writing stills the sound of speech by breaking up and dismembering a vertical immediacy into a horizontal presence. Then vertical presence recedes behind and before the impacting center of voice and in that expanding horizon an immediate identity passes into simile and metaphor. Nevertheless, a tension is present in most or all of the synoptic parables which gives witness to this process of dismemberment and reversal, a tension which is most evident in the chasm which opens up between the story or antistory of the parable and the allegorical interpretation which is sometimes present in the synoptic text. It is precisely in this tension that the original intention of the parable becomes manifest. While that intention cannot be fully manifest in this tension, and cannot be so if only because of the silence of writing, it is nonetheless true that a trace of a primary process of reversal is present here, and in that trace we can detect an echo of a now distant immediacy.

We must never lose sight of the fact that the early Christian communities created the Gospel as a literary genre, and thereby made possible the conjunction or coinherence of action or plot and *logia* or saying. Nothing quite like this was previously present in either Greece or Israel, for only with the birth of Christianity does a speech appear and sound which is simultaneously praxis and voice. Christian anamnesis is not a mere remembrance or recollection, it is rather a renewal or re-presentation of an identity which is originally act and voice at once. True, this original identity was dismembered by both the cultus of the churches and by the texts of the Gospels. But this dismemberment was not complete, as witness the fact that the Gospels establish a horizon of meaning wherein *logia* can speak within the context of life and world. While the field of this actuality is repeatedly turned askew by the ecclesiastical motives and intentions of the Gospel writers or schools, it is never wholly dislodged in the parables, even if it often threatens to disappear from view. The stark contrast between the parables and the legends of the Gospels is striking evidence of a dichotomous presence in the New Testament which again and again tends to disrupt and deconstruct the text. Perhaps the continual if subterranean presence of such a threat of deconstruction is a primary source of both the power and the actuality of the Gospel texts.

What is most manifestly missing from the true parable is the vision and language of myth. This is a striking phenomenon, for both myth and parable conjoin the world and the sacred and each establishes a continuum between human and cosmic identity. Yet that continuum is horizontal in myth, it stretches out into a visionary plane, whereas it is immediate and vertical in parable. Myth distances both the speaker and the hearer from the moment or center of voice, a distance expanding into the horizon of vision. But parable contracts attention into the presence or moment at hand, a presence whose very immediacy resists and opposes the horizontal movement of vision. Pure parable embodies an auditory as opposed to a visual presence, an immediate sounding which commands and effects a total attention. One hears a parable, and does so even in reading, for parable sounds or speaks an immediate presence. True, that presence is the presence of world, and the presence of that world which is immediately and commonly at hand. Yet, in parable, world overwhelms the hearer, and overwhelms the hearer in its immediacy, allowing little or no room for the distancing of vision. Here, world speaks only in its immediacy, only in its being immediately at hand, an at-handedness which itself is eschatological judgment.

All too naturally, parable expands into allegory in memory and tradition, and is thereby transposed into a visual and mythical language. However, in the synoptic Gospels, as opposed to the Fourth Gospel, such mythical language is obviously derived and secondhand. No attentive reader could possibly confuse the language of allegorical interpretation with the speech of parabolic voice here. The overwhelming difference between parabolic and allegorical language not only bespeaks the distance between parable and allegory, but also the distance between memory and speech. While that distance may well be crossed in the Gospel of John, it clearly is not in the allegorical language of the synoptic Gospels, and the very artificiality and secondhandedness of that language gives witness to the loss or dilution of voice. With and in that loss there is not only a loss of the original speaker, but a loss of world as well. No longer is world incarnate in the voice of speech, just as world is no longer immediately at hand. But a manifest and parallel distancing of both world and speech gives witness to an original presence of an immediate continuum between voice and world.

The very everydayness of true parabolic language bespeaks an immediate presence of world in voice. Parabolic enactment occurs on earth and not in heaven, in "flesh" as opposed to "spirit." Now is the time of decision, and this nowness reverses every trace of a beyond which is only beyond. So likewise, there occurs here a reversal of a world which is merely and only world. World now stands forth in its immediacy, and that immediacy is itself the time of decision. Now voice itself is praxis, the praxis of a world come of age. At no point in this immediacy is either world or voice only itself, for each is charged with a total and eschatological presence. In that presence there is an immediate continuum between the actuality of both world and voice, and therein is embodied a judgment which is simultaneously both eschatological and here and now. This is a simultaneity which is lost with the advent of metaphor and allegory, for metaphor and allegory break up the immediacy of a totally actual present by establishing a horizontal distance between language and world.

This is a distance which is absent from pure parabolic speech, for pure parabolic speech does not speak about the world, if only because it does not speak of or about anything whatsoever. On the contrary, here world speaks in voice itself, and as voice as well. True parabolic speech is the speech of world itself, a speech wherein and whereby world is totally actual and immediately at hand. Then speech is world and world is speech at once. Such speech calls its hearer out of a world which is silent and apart and into a world which is embodied in the full actuality of voice. The silence of the world ends in parabolic speech, and ends because parabolic speech gives utterance to the full actuality of time and world. It is precisely the absence of metaphorical and allegorical distancing which makes possible this full and immediate presence of speech. Then the act of speech is an incarnation of world, an incarnation of world in the pure immediacy of voice.

SELF-EMBODIMENT AND ESCHATOLOGICAL SPEECH

One of the most difficult problems posed by modern New Testament scholarship is the identity of eschatological speech. We now know that eschatological speech, or eschatological act and speech, is the originating center of both Christianity and the New Testament. But what is eschatological speech? It has become common to attempt to resolve this problem by way of establishing a dichotomy between eschatological speech and mythical language. In its Bultmannian expression, this takes the form of posing a dichotomy between a subjective or existential eschatological faith and an objective or cosmic mythical vision. Then a consistent and comprehensive demythologizing of a cosmic mythical vision is an eschatological or existential expression of faith. Thereby eschatological becomes identified as existential and the incarnate or the Christian Word becomes identified as the existential Word. Then the center of the New Testament becomes

eschatological faith and its alien periphery either apocalyptic
or Gnostic mythology. Quite naturally this "subjective" or existential form of demythologizing has had an immense impact upon modern theology, for it seems to be our only way of
bringing together a modern historical interpretation of the
New Testament with a contemporary meaning of its faith
and Word.

But this option is closing as existential language is already
receding into our historical past and mythical and cosmic
language is being reborn in our midst. Language and speech
have also gained a new and comprehensive identity, and
surely the time is at hand to conjoin the eschatological with
a primal identity of speech. Once again our fundamental
problem is the theological identity of Kingdom of God. And
here the synoptic parables must continue to remain at or near
the center of our analysis. Clearly the parables of Jesus are
parables of the Kingdom of God, and thus they are an expression of Jesus' eschatological proclamation. But the Kingdom
of God is not the subject of these parables in an ordinary
sense, for in that sense they have no subject at all. That is to
say, they are without a subject which can clearly be delinea-
ted or sharply distinguished from anything else. The parables
of Jesus do not point to the Kingdom of God in the sense of
pointing at an object; that is just the possibility which is
hereby foreclosed.

In one sense the parables do point either to the presence or
to the immediately coming presence of the Kingdom of God.
Indeed, this very ambiguity makes manifest an essential identity of the Kingdom in the parables, for it is both present and
future and yet neither present nor future. Our temporal
distinctions break down upon impact with the parables, and

so likewise do our spatial distinctions. The Kingdom of God, in the parables as a whole, is neither "here" nor "there," neither above nor below, neither before nor behind. Again and again the parables make clear that it is just such distinctions which divert our attention from the Kingdom of God. Thus a paradox is present here, and perhaps a pure paradox, for the parables seem both to speak and to be silent simultaneously. One might say that they speak with perfect clarity even while saying nothing which we can truly either define or repeat. There is a pure simplicity present here, a simplicity making the parable immediately understandable to everyone who hears it, and yet its meaning breaks down when it is expressed in nonparabolic language.

Now we know or can imagine that the pure parable is intended to engage a total attention, an attention so total as to hear and be aware of nothing but this speech. Hence the immediate actuality of parabolic speech, an actuality making all possible meaning and identity incarnate here and now. This is the actuality which is diluted in metaphorical meaning and then lost in allegory. But it is an actuality which is also diluted and lost when the parable is transposed into anything which we can know as plot or story. The ending of the true parable is not simply a surprise, or even a shock; rather, it shatters everything which is recognizable as meaning or identity to us. Yet the parable does not culminate in a simple silence or emptiness. On the contrary, its ending evokes and embodies an actuality which is indubitable, and not only indubitable but overwhelming to its hearer as well. Then the hearer can be understood to lose every identity and meaning which he or she initially brings to the parable. But that meaning is lost not simply by being negated, but rather by being reversed. And it is reversed in the very context of the parabolic situation and by the very movement of the parabolic tale or image. So it is that the attention which the parable invites and commands culminates in an explosion of the hearer, and an explosion which is enacted by the hearer as a consequence of hearing this speech.

It is not difficult to associate such an explosion with eschatological judgment. But it is not only an existential or subjective judgment, it is a cosmic or "objective" judgment as well, or a judgment which transforms and reverses all actual and possible meaning. True, it is our identity which here comes under judgment. But it is our total identity which is assaulted by the parable, and this occurs through a reversal of a whole world of meaning. And that reversal occurs in the actual hearing of the hearer, a hearing in which the hearer is totally engaged. This is not a judgment which awaits the hearer, or falls upon the hearer, or even happens to the hearer. It is, far rather, a judgment which is realized in the actuality of hearing itself, and realized by the hearer in the hearer's own act of hearing. Thereby hearing passes into speech itself, for it realizes a new and total identity of the hearer, and does so by way of the hearer's own act of hearing. Nor is that act simply a self-destructive or self-negating act. On the contrary, it is a self-realizing act, an act which realizes an actuality and an immediacy which otherwise is absent.

Within the context of the world and sound of parabolic speech, it is possible to speak of speech itself as the negation of mythical vision. Indeed, it is the negation, transcendence, or reversal of vision itself, a negation of all horizons and planes lying outside of and beyond the pure immediacy of speech. The silence of distance vanishes in that pure immediacy, and it does not simply vanish, it rather passes into speech. Then Kingdom of God is not distant and apart; it speaks, and fully speaks, in the actuality of voice. Then world is not simply and only world; it, too, is embodied in voice. Then we are not simply the hearer of world and Word, we speak both Word and world in hearing this voice. Thereby parabolic speech issues in a hearing whereby and wherein the Kingdom of God is immediately at hand. And it is at hand in the actuality of hearing itself, a hearing transposing the silence of both God and world into the immediate actuality of Kingdom of God. Therefore parabolic speech culminates in a total hearing, a hearing whose own immediate actuality is the self-realization or self-embodiment of speech.

Voice itself is the originating center of the New Testament, a voice which actually speaks an immediate and total presence. That presence sounds in a purely parabolic speech, and its sounding dissolves all boundaries between a "here" and a "there," thereby fusing or uniting the "here" and the "there" into a continuum of immediate actuality. But that actuality is a spoken actuality, an actuality which fully and actually speaks, and therefore it is worlds or aeons removed from the cosmic totality of archaic myth. If myth in its fullest expressions knows a center which is everywhere, voice in its purest expressions speaks a center which is here and now. And that center is everywhere only by being here and now, only by its actual and immediate embodiment in speech. That embodiment shatters every mythical and visual identity, every speakable distinction, and does so by way of an eschatological or total judgment which is present in voice alone. Here, voice is the self-embodiment of speech, and the self-embodiment of a speech which is total or all in all. But it is all in all only by being a total rupturing of silence, only by bringing a final end to all identity which does not or cannot speak.

In the presence of this judgment it is impossible to speak of Kingdom of God as such. Impossible, that is, to speak of a singular or particular identity of Kingdom of God. We might say that here every mythical or visual identity of Kingdom of God comes to an end, and comes to an end because here every mythical or visual horizon is shattered by the pure immediacy of speech. No longer does transcendence stand or appear apart, just as no longer does world stand and appear as world in our midst. Neither God nor world is now speakable as God or world alone, and they are unspeakable because now it is impossible to speak or envision any identity which is only itself. The fullness of voice or speech dissolves every identity lying beyond its own immediacy, and thereby perishes every identity which is isolated and self-enclosed. Here is negation and reversal in its purest form, in its most radical expression, and it is so because it brings an end to all possible individual meaning and identity. That end occurs in the fullness of voice or speech, for in that fullness there is a total negation of all silent identity. This occurs by way of the collapse and reversal of every horizontal or visual continuum, and in that collapse and judgment is realized the full advent of Word and of Word alone.

THE PRETEXTUAL IDENTITY OF SPEECH

Not only is it true that Jesus left us no documents or writing of any kind, but it has also now been firmly established that nowhere in the Gospels may we find a single sentence which we can treat with confidence as having its sole source in Jesus.

We simply have no *ipsissima verba* of Jesus, nor of any other ancient prophet. Theology was prepared for this historical realization by a theology of the Word which radically distinguishes Word from words. We have been given and are called to the Word of faith, but the Word of faith is not to be confused with the words of the Bible. Biblical language expresses and embodies the Word, but it is not simply to be identified with the Word. Yes, Jesus was a prophet proclaiming the advent or dawning of the Kingdom of God, and it is of vital importance both historically and theologically to realize that he was the first prophet to do so. But we have no mode of access to the actual words with which he celebrated this advent, just as we have no way of recovering the exact actions with which he embodied and realized his proclamation. While this does not distinguish Jesus from any other ancient prophet, even including Confucius and Socrates, to say nothing of Lao Tzu and the Buddha, it does mean that we must wholly repudiate every temptation to identify Jesus with any Gospel text or texts.

Only with the advent of the Enlightenment and the birth of the modern historical consciousness did the awareness dawn of real and seemingly uncrossable distinctions within the New Testament itself, not only distinctions between the Epistles and the Gospels, but also real distinctions between the Gospels themselves, and most particularly so between the Fourth Gospel and the synoptics. It was this latter distinction which posed the greatest theological problem because it was the Gospel of John which not only most deeply influenced, but also most decisively shaped orthodox Christian faith and doctrine. Now it became fully apparent that this Gospel simply could not be reconciled with the other three, and the synoptics are manifestly far closer historically to the original Jesus. While the nineteenth-century quest for the historical Jesus seemingly culminated in failure, it fundamentally resulted in resounding success, for it definitively established the historical identity of Jesus as an apocalyptic or eschatological prophet, an identity which to this day has not been challenged but only reinforced. Biblical scholars and theologians, however, are commonly unaware that the eschatological identity of Jesus had earlier been realized imaginatively by Blake and conceptually by Hegel, and in each case breakthroughs occurred which realized the full advent of modernity. Indeed, apocalyptic forms of Christianity had always known this identity, and radical expressions of Christian mysticism had long since realized a fully interior yet total Word which is the mystical equivalent of an apocalyptic or eschatological Word.

It is noteworthy that neither in apocalypticism, nor in Christian mysticism, nor in the highest expressions of the Christian imagination, is there a centering or focusing upon the words of Jesus as such. Just as liturgy and ritual invariably subordinate word to action or rite, so likewise faith and the imagination inevitably transcend both the limits and the identities of word or words. To confine the identity of Jesus to words or text is to lose that identity, a loss which has occurred again and again in Christian history, but most obviously so in the modern world. Hence, in attempting to recover the parabolic language of Jesus we must not confuse that language with the words of the synoptic texts. Nor may we allow the form or forms of the synoptic parables to determine or mold our sense of the original identity of the parable, for it is now clear that these forms or structures are movements away from the original parables. But if we can see that the parable itself is a reversal of all given or manifest meaning and identity, and that the synoptic parables move in the direction of reversing the original parables, then in this movement of reversing reversal we can apprehend a decisive way of returning to an original parabolic language. Therein we can also see that the words of text are a reversal of Word, a reversal resurrecting an originally negated meaning and identity.

Furthermore, if we can see that parable itself is antistory or antiplot, that it is a reversal of the forward or unilinear movement of plot, or a negation of all manifest or given forms or structures of narrative, then we can be given a further means of recovering the all too elusive identity of parabolic speech. There would appear to be substantial critical agreement that it is those parables in the synoptics with either the least narrative or the most discordant or baffling narrative structure which are closest to the original parables of Jesus, and we can also see that in the Gospels clarity of narrative structure and convertibility into allegorical interpretation seemingly go hand in hand. Since it is now virtually unanimously accepted that the allegorical interpretations are the end products of a process of parabolic transformation or reversal, then it is clear that formal or narrative structures which are most open to allegorical interpretation are most distant from the original parables. If we go further, and understand simile and metaphor as dilutions of parabolic speech, then we can understand that the very act of writing deeply transforms a purely parabolic language. By necessity, writing expands into a visual horizon the original immediacy of speech. Thereby that immediacy is not only diluted but also transformed, as its original centeredness is not only expanded into a horizontal structure, but is also thereby given a new form and identity. As the intonations and modulations of voice pass into grammatical and syntactical structure, an original actual immediacy progressively becomes frozen not simply into a static form, but also into a form which reverses the original immediacy of voice.

Such judgments about writing and text are increasingly being accepted and affirmed, and this is occurring among a wide variety of biblical scholars and theologians, and certainly it is in part a response to the widespread recognition that we have long since lost the ability to read text as Scripture. It is highly significant that the Protestant recovery of the Bible, and the Protestant *sola scriptura*, was and is an expression of a kerygmatic form of faith and witness, a preached or oral embodiment of faith. Once the Bible is detached or dissociated from this speaking or oral ground, it increasingly loses its power as Scripture, and becomes manifest as a text like any other. But the intrinsic power of the parables was lost at the very beginning of Christian history, and this loss was simply petrified as the parables were thereafter understood as little more than moral examples or mythical allegories. Then the parables were rediscovered or resurrected in the twentieth century, and above all in the late twentieth century, and by a scholarly and theological world which whether directly or indirectly had been deeply affected by the literary revolutions of the twentieth century. The truth is that Kafka discovered the power of parabolic language long before it was unearthed by biblical scholarship, and he did so unassisted by the work of theologians or New Testament scholars.

But Kafka's parabolic discourse, which is present not only in his parables, but also in his stories, novels, and journals, is both the product and a ground of a literary revolution, a revolution transforming the very identity of literature. One decisive sign of this revolution is that our truly modern literature is literary and nonliterary at once, it is a fully literary language even as it is a fully everyday or common language, as witness Kafka. Then the classical literary genres break down, and poetry passes into prose, even as prose passes into poetry, and epic and tragedy while unquestionably present are simply unrecognizable as such. This is the situation in which we have rediscovered the parables of Jesus, a situation in which true everyday language is poetry and prose at once, and comic and tragic at once. Thereby literary language has returned or become open once again to its original oral source, and voice itself has been reenacted in text, even if such a reenactment gives text the form of antitext. Once such a literary revolution has occurred, a text which is manifest only as text will have little literary power, and little human power as well. Hence the realization that true or pure parabolic language is a preliterary or nonliterary language has given parabolic language a whole new power and immediacy for us. But that immediacy dissipates when parable is identified wholly with its textual form, for if the Gospels preserved the parables of Jesus, they were also vehicles by which parabolic language was diluted and reversed.

Chapter Two

THE
ANONYMITY
OF
GOD

THE ANONYMITY OF SELFHOOD

It is manifest that an anonymous speech and identity abounds among us, and perhaps never more so than today. We know this all too well if only because we have not only evolved, but also have become dominated by a form of language which annuls or dissolves what once was present and real as a unique and individual form of selfhood or self-consciousness. This is true not only of our scientific, technological, and bureaucratic language, but of our poetic and conceptual language as well. Nevertheless, ours is not a simply or literally anonymous world. For it is not possible to imagine, even in fantasy or reverie, a literal anonymity. And we know all too well that identity of some kind, and of multiple kinds, is firmly established in our world. Our problem is that the deepest and most powerful identity in our world is incompatible with and alien to what we once knew and realized as identity, and most particularly so as selfhood or self-identity. Anonymity is virtually a living presence among us, and not only among us, but also deeply within us, a presence beyond which neither our artists nor our thinkers can penetrate. So pervasive is this presence, indeed, that we can no longer either imagine or conceive a region beyond such anonymity. Moreover, the anonymity which we are ever more fully coming to know is a total presence, a presence pervading all our modes of both speech and silence. Let us speak of it then as a totality. Images of totality permeate the history of religions and mythology, and these have again and again been resurrected by the imagination. Dante's *Comedy*, for example, presents us with a master image of totality, an image or total image wherein heaven, the cosmos, and hell are not only integral and integrated worlds, but wherein everything whatsoever within these worlds, even including history, politics, and psychology, is a fully orchestrated and comprehensive order which simultaneously both mirrors and embodies a universal totality. In a parallel even if far less comprehensive manner and mode, the late triptychs of Hieronymus Bosch fully integrate the realms of heaven, earth, and hell, although this is an interior as opposed to a cosmic totality, and a totality consumed by the dominance of hell. Therein we might be tempted to name Bosch rather than Luther as the founder of the Reformation, but less than a hundred years later, and above all in the dramatic poetry of Shakespeare, although fully foreshadowed in the portraits of Leonardo, an autonomous self-consciousness triumphs with such power as to foreclose the possibility of another Dante.

As Hegel taught us, the owl of Minerva spreads its wings only with the falling of the dusk, and only in the twilight of self-consciousness have we learned that self-consciousness has a historical beginning, even as it is now apparently undergoing a historical end. That beginning lies in Christianity, initially in Paul, but decisively in Augustine, for it is not until Augustine that we can discover an understanding or even a full awareness of self-consciousness. The Augustine who was most responsible for the creation of our dominant theological understanding of God succeeded theologically only by first creating the literary genre of autobiography, and thereby and thereafter realizing a truly new and personal identity of selfhood. While Augustinianism has commonly been a primary ground of Western mysticism, it was also reborn in Protestantism, and not only in Luther and Calvin, but also in Milton and Rembrandt. The portraits and self-portraits of Rembrandt are perhaps the clearest embodiments of a new and solitary self-consciousness, a unique self-consciousness which is both the creator and the mirror of its world. And in *Paradise Lost* even Satan and Adam, and perhaps Christ himself, are reenacted and reborn by way of a majestic and awesome poetic language which is nevertheless the reflection and expression of a unique and autonomous selfhood and self-consciousness. But the Hegel who understood so deeply that self-consciousness is the primal ground of the modern age, and of the postclassical Western or Christian consciousness as well, was also the Hegel who conceptually realized the end of self-consciousness, an ending which was subjectively recreated, but with infinitely greater interior power, in Kierkegaard and Nietzsche.

It might be said that self-consciousness is itself a totality in the modern world, but if so it is a dynamic and self-realizing totality, and a totality which realizes itself by ever more fully and progressively transforming and dissolving its original identity. For example, Proust's vision of time recaptured is a vision of the presence of eternity in a real, concrete, and actual moment of self-consciousness. But, here, time can be recaptured as eternity only when a concrete moment of time has passed through a process of oblivion in consciousness, therein it is isolated from the vicissitudes of self-consciousness and preserved in a pure state by being forgotten, and thence can be resurrected as eternity when a contingent and accidental event occurs wherein there is a coincidence between a present and actual moment of self-consciousness and the now forgotten and hence pure but once actual original moment. Yet this deeply modern presence of eternity can occur only as a consequence of the loss or disappearance of all the assurances and certainties of self-consciousness. Thus we find the paradox that *Remembrance of Things Past* is at once the deepest orchestration of selfhood in modern fiction even while that orchestration is itself the very arena and avenue whereby and wherein our deepest selfhood passes into oblivion and itself as selfhood becomes wholly anonymous. Proust's novel is in part a reflection of Monet's landscapes, and if only through Proust we can realize that the immense power of Monet's later painting, and most particularly so his late water lilies, derives from his success in actually seeing, and inducing us to see, a total presence, even if that presence is wholly anonymous. We are present here, and present by seeing the water lilies, even if that presence forecloses what we once saw and knew ourselves to be.

Both the modern imagination and modern science, as well as truly modern thinking, have conducted profound and comprehensive assaults upon both the exterior and interior forms of our given identities. And one way by which this assault has occurred is through the interior realization of anonymity, an anonymity both paralleling and reflecting the exterior realization of a total anonymity in modern science. Theologically, we may identify this realization as judgment, and also as self-judgment. Few theologians, however, have taken note of the biblical ground and source of that awesome and all-pervading guilt and self-judgment which have so dominated the modern mind and sensibility. Nowhere else is there such a clear and decisive link between the biblical world and our world. We might also note that, if it was Augustine who created the literary genre of autobiography, it was Blake who created the literary genre of apocalypse. Just as the *Confessions* made possible an initial voyage into the depths of selfhood which made manifest the genesis of self-hood as an epiphany of the personal presence and identity of God, then so likewise do *Milton* and *Jerusalem* make manifest a cosmic and total self-judgment as the realization of a final epiphany of an apocalyptic God. In these apocalyptic epics an ultimate self-judgment is finally "self-annihilation," wherein an apocalyptic night of judgment passes into an apocalyptic day of forgiveness and joy. If a fully personal or self-conscious identity was first realized by Augustine, then it is in Blake that we may observe the first modern expression of the full self-negation of that identity. Self-judgment lies at the very center of each of these realizations of the identity of selfhood, and each shatters and transforms a previously given and established form of selfhood.

Historically, the genesis of what we have known as self-consciousness occurs in Paul's meditations upon guilt, where-in the actualization of self-judgment realizes the initial birth of a fully personal self-consciousness. That consciousness knows itself as fallen, hence self-consciousness is here a guilty consciousness, or quite simply a bad conscience. That bad conscience realizes its own interior identity in the Augustinian transformation of consciousness, and as a result of that transformation, or self-transformation, previous forms of selfhood here disappear from view. Then these forms of selfhood appear as unreal or anonymous to self-consciousness. Apart from the interior realization of self-consciousness, self-consciousness itself is neither actually present nor actually absent. But once it is present, it is irresistibly present, or is so until it fully realizes itself. Not until Shakespeare will the depths and breadths of this self-consciousness be celebrated or explored, but as that exploration and self-exploration of consciousness evolved, earlier forms and expressions of consciousness receded into a night of anonymity. From this perspective, anonymity is a consequence of judgment, and of self-judgment, a self-judgment which is a self-negation. Not surprisingly, guilt is a primary if not the primary language of self-consciousness, and this is true not only of Augustine, Luther, and Kierkegaard, but also of Shakespeare, Nietzsche, and Beckett. At no other point has modern imaginative language so openly realized its biblical source.

If we could imagine a line running from Paul to Beckett, and could understand this line as representing the historical movement of self-consciousness, then we might be able to imagine such a history as embodying the autobiography of self-consciousness, beginning with its birth in initial self-judgment and culminating with its death in total self-judgment. Both before and after this line there is only anonymity, at least from the point of view of self-consciousness. We might also observe that after innumerable evolving cycles and gyrations the line finally returns to its initial configuration. For the nihilism which most Christians find in Beckett is found by most non-Christians in Paul. Both are apocalyptic visionaries, and both are obsessed by chaos, guilt, and self-judgment. Indeed, for both the very form and identity of self-consciousness is identical with self-judgment. Yet in Paul self-consciousness initially comes into existence and in Beckett it seemingly comes to an end. True, Beckett's contemporaries, or the great bulk of us, proceed as though nothing has happened, but so likewise did Paul's. Paul knew that the end of history was at hand, and so, too, does Beckett, and not only Beckett but a host of modern visionaries. If an ancient form of selfhood came to an end with the birth of self-consciousness, then a modern form of selfhood may well be coming to an end today, and in that ending self-consciousness itself passes into a total anonymity.

THE MYSTERY AND UNKNOWABILITY OF GOD

Commonly, we think of the mystery of God as the unknowability of God. This can and has gone hand in hand with a confident faith in God, and many theologians have affirmed that true faith in God can be noted by its realization of the pure or total unknowability of God. Unknowability then becomes the primary attribute of God, and the primary attribute for faith. Hence Kierkegaard could insist that it is precisely the unknowability or mystery of God which most fundamentally distinguishes faith from paganism, and this primary Kierkegaardian thesis has been widely echoed in our own century. Here, mystery or unknowability is the primary identity of God for us, and that mystery is the deepest and most ultimate source of meaning and identity for us. Thus, when the mystery of God appears in this form it can be a living ground of theology, and a ground reflecting the knowledge of God in faith. For, in this sense, the unknowability of God is a consequence of the true or radical transcendence of God, a transcendence which can only truly be known in faith.

Obviously there is an overwhelming and uncrossable distance between an unknowability which is a mark or sign of the transcendence of God and an unknowability which is simply and only unknowability. So, likewise, there is a comparable distinction between a mystery which is a mystery of transcendence and a mystery which is wholly and only mystery. Transcendent mystery is a decisive sign of a transcendent identity, an identity which is spoken when the name of God is uttered or pronounced in faith. But a mystery which is wholly and only a mystery cannot be spoken or evoked as such, and must therefore perforce remain silent. We can sense the truth of this judgment by noting the distinction between a negative attribute of God, or a negative naming of God, and the absence of all naming whatsoever. We are also aware of the distinction between an iconoclastic art in which the absence of all images of God or the sacred nevertheless evokes a sacred identity, such as the art of early Buddhism and Islam, and an art which forecloses the very possibility of sacred images or identity, as is true of the great bulk of modern art. Hence there is a clear and radical distinction between an unknowability which is the consequence of the presence of a transcendent or mysterious identity and an unknowability which is the consequence of the absence of all identity as such.

Even poets and philosophers have now ceased speaking of God, and while their silence has been heard by many theologians as grace, it would more clearly appear to be a consequence of the presence of a new unknowability of God. We have surely entered a world, and above all a language world, in which there is not only the absence of all names or images of God, but more deeply absent the very possibility of naming or identifying God as God. God is truly nameless in such a world, and thus here we can properly speak of the anonymity of God. Yet if we know ourselves only by knowing God, and this has been affirmed by Christians as diverse as Augustine and Descartes, to say nothing of Tertullian and Dostoevski or Paul and Blake, then to know the anonymity of God is to know the anonymity of selfhood, and thereby we can realize yet another ground of our contemporary anonymity. Certainly the anonymity which we know has a ground going beyond all which is identifiable to us as either world or self-identity, and does so because anonymity is deeply and profoundly present at the very center of our language and speech. This is a center which Christians long have identified with God, or with the presence or impact of God, for it is the grounding center or source of all meaning and identity. But if an anonymous identity is grounded in an anonymous source or center, and both identity and source are actually and truly anonymous, then it would seem that such anonymity is purely and simply unknowable.

All too naturally many theologians have returned to a classical mystical language to speak of our world and situation, and have employed such images as eclipse, the cloud of unknowing, and the dark night of the soul. But these images are fraught with difficulty for us if only because, in terms of their own language worlds, each of them presupposes and posits the potential presence or actuality of its own opposite or contrary. Eclipse, cloud, and night are here meaningful and real only in terms of the potential and finally total presence of their contraries or opposites, and were employed by the mystics to speak of the prelude or preparation for full union or coinherence with God. However, in a situation in which images of God no longer appear to be even potentially possible for us, all such mystical language breaks down. Or breaks down in terms of its original language world, a world in which God is not wholly anonymous, or is anonymous only in that penultimate and purgatorial state which is directed to the dissolution or erasure of all dark or fallen images of God. True, classical mystics may have individually and interiorly realized an empty or negative state which has become historically universal in the modern world, as Hegel divined. For the depths of what Hegel understood as the unhappy consciousness and self-alienation are both the birth pangs of true modernity and the initial but decisive expressions of a full or pure self-consciousness. But there is little sign or evidence that a grace is thereby realized in our world which we can mystically name as a totality of light.

What we do find in our world is a radical iconoclasm revolving about a thoroughgoing negation of all our given images of both deity and humanity. Hence, the Mahayana Buddhist category of *sunya*, voidness or emptiness, would seem to have been born or reborn in our midst, and reborn at just those points where the modern consciousness is most actual and real. Yet Mahayana Buddhism dawned and dawns in a purely mystical movement or epiphany which is wholly negative and wholly positive at once. So much is this the case that here it is impossible to distinguish positive and negative poles, and while the language of Mahayana Buddhism presents itself or is manifest to us as a wholly negative language, this is manifestly because enlightenment or release must inevitably appear in a negative form and identity to a conditioned and differentiated consciousness. What is most distinctive about the language of Mahayana Buddhism for us is that it presents and realizes itself in a purely and totally negative mode. Yet it is precisely the act of total negation which here realizes total liberation, precisely the full and actual realization that everything whatsoever is totally void or empty of meaning or identity which realizes full or total enlightenment. The Buddhist symbol of *Sunyata* evokes a plenitude of emptiness, but an emptiness which is a totality of freedom or grace, even if these words must bear a wholly negative or nihilistic meaning and identity to our minds and sensibility.

Nevertheless, Mallarmé could envision pure nothingness as a mystical plenitude of grace, and Nietzsche envisioned and enacted eternal recurrence as a total movement or act which is simultaneously a nihilistic negation of all meaning and identity and a total affirmation or *Yes*-saying of triumphant joy. Surely something like a Buddhist *sunya* or *Sunyata* is present in our world, even if in a hidden or reversed form and identity. If we can become open to this possibility, then we can become open to the possibility that the anonymity of God need not be for us a simple or literal unknowability, but rather a new and total unknowability released by the negation and erasure of all our previous images of God. Genuine iconoclasm presupposes the presence of an affirmation making possible its negation, as can be seen clearly in Buddhism, Yahwism, and Islam. If a radical iconoclasm is present in our world, then its total negation of all names and images must be grounded in a pure or total act of affirmation, even if we cannot yet theologically conceive or envision such an act. Already, Melville's *Moby Dick*, the first symbolical or mythical novel, has initiated us into a new anonymity of God. The whiteness of the whale is as awesome as the majesty of the Creator, and it, too, is a transcendent mystery, a mystery making transcendence present to us. But its transcendence is a nameless transcendence, or a wholly empty and negative transcendence, and is so most forcefully when Melville induces us to see and name Moby Dick. While the whiteness of the whale can readily be construed as an overwhelmingly powerful image of the anonymity of God, its very whiteness or emptiness can also be realized as a polar power which is negative and positive at once. For if we are crushed and overwhelmed by the awesome presence of the whale, we can realize through the epic action of this novel the dawning of a movement which promises a breakthrough into our deepest depths.

A NEW ANONYMITY

Far Eastern landscape painting initially startles us if only because we cannot readily identify the human presences which might be present within it. Soon we realize that these presences are enriched by their apparent absence and that our inability here to see a singularly human form is precisely what makes possible our ability to see the fullness of a human identity which otherwise is invisible to us. So, likewise, the radical transformation or disappearance of the human face in cubist and abstract painting is not simply the consequence of a negative vision of the end of humanity, but rather a truly new and positive vision of an integral selfhood which is organically united with an exterior world of time and space. Both God and man seem to be wholly absent from Monet's landscapes, but once we realize that we are confronting a total presence in his paintings, then we can be aware that this may well be a presence comprehending not only nature, but also both the human and the divine. If we can apprehend the possibility of total vision, we may thereby recognize that the anonymity of both God and man may well be an essential ground for the realization of such vision. Or, at least, an essential ground for a movement from a vision centered in an interior and individual identity to a cosmic and universal vision.

Quite significantly, the power of archaic or prehistoric art was discovered by the West at just the moment when the dominant Western images of God and man were undergoing a full process of either dissolution or transformation. That vast region of consciousness lying on the yonder side of Abraham had long been unreal to us, and unreal because of the historical consequences of an original naming of God, a naming which gradually but progressively realized an individual and personal center of consciousness. Once that center burst asunder, as it did in the nineteenth century, then an original primordial identity came into view, and it was an identity lacking either a transcendent or an immanent center. Yet modern painting is obviously not a simple repetition or resurrection of archaic art, just as modern literature is clearly not a simple reenactment or renewal of archaic myth. While there may well be decisive parallels between archaic art and myth and modern art and literature, there are also decisive differences, and one such fundamental difference is the virtual absence of a distinct form of the holy or the sacred from truly modern language and vision.

At first glance cubism seems to be a resurrection of archaic art, but we soon realize that the faces in cubist art are not archaic faces, just as the objects of cubist painting do not embody a primordial presence. The faces of the women of Picasso's *Les Demoiselles d'Avignon*, while exhibiting a progression from naturalistic to violently distorted visages, embody even if in a reverse form the primal impact of an interior and individual center of consciousness. Just as cubism was initially made possible by Cézanne, it carries forward the tradition of Western painting, even if the object of that painting is now realized in a truly new form and identity. Perhaps we will someday come to understand that there is no greater distance between Picasso and Leonardo than there is between Leonardo and Giotto, for just as the portraits of the High Renaissance transcended the form established by the human icons of Giotto, modern painting has broken through the forms established by the Renaissance. Yet it is crucial to note that it has broken through them and not simply dissolved them, for if modern art has become a universal art in our world, it nevertheless has never ceased to embody its Western ground and origin. Even fully abstract painting is the realization of a distinctively and uniquely Western object, and just as it may parallel the coinherence of subject and object in quantum physics, it also realizes that pure objectivity foreseen by Kierkegaard in which there is a total absence of the truly individual subject. When fully realized, as in the late paintings of Barnett Newman, abstract art seems to pass into nonart, for it dissolves the frame of the easel, passing into the world beyond it, and that world is a purely and totally anonymous world.

Our anonymity must not be confused with an archaic anonymity. And it cannot be so confused if only because we know that a modern anonymity, as opposed to an archaic anonymity, is truly and actually our own. We recognize ourselves in modern art as we do not in archaic art, for we know that a purely abstract and seemingly formless identity is deeply present within ourselves, and we actually realize this identity in confronting an abstract painting. Nor do we recognize such a painting as simply a negative image of ourselves. On the contrary, a real power is present in modern art, a power which we seek, and it is not inconsequential that our museums have become sanctuaries, and have become so only after the advent of modern art. Theologically, we must identify this power as a holy power, even if it is not visible in a holy or sacred form. At times this power is visible as a sacred power, as in many of the paintings of van Gogh, but then it is always a destructive and chaotic power, as it violently asaults the last bastions of an interior center of consciousness. It is noteworthy that, when modern painting seemingly has a wholly liberating or redemptive effect, as in Monet and Cézanne, it bears no signs of the holy, and in no way whatsoever exhibits even a shadow of God. This does not mean, of course, that God and the sacred are necessarily absent from these paintings. But it does mean that if they are present they are present wholly apart from their given and historical forms and identities.

Now if we must perforce recognize that we ourselves are present, and present in our innermost identity, in modern art, then we must also recognize that any such identity is profoundly distant from any form of a unique and autonomous self-consciousness. Must we then not also conclude that if God is present in a uniquely modern vision then God cannot be present, or cannot manifestly or recognizably be present, as the sovereign, transcendent, and personal Lord? True, something like images of transcendent lordship appear in modern painting, as in the late landscapes of van Gogh. While overwelming in its effect upon the viewer, and over-whelming as a numinous power, such lordship is never here associated with a personal identity or source, but rather with a faceless and primal chaos. That primal chaos does evoke the imagery of archaic art, but unlike archaic art, or, at least, its non-Mayan expressions, these all too modern images of transcendent power are wholly dissociated from any assuag-ing or atoning power. We may be tempted to name this transcendent power as Moby Dick, but as opposed both to Melville's novel and the earlier paintings of van Gogh, in such landscapes as *The Plain Near Auvers* and *Wheat Field with Crows* a transcendent chaos has come so totally into view as to dissolve the possibility of any other presence. Here, it is sim-ply not possible to say that any form of personal deity lies behind or beneath these surfaces. Yet the sheer power of these paintings is not simply a brutal power, nor even solely a purely chaotic power, for we actually see this power, and in that very vision darkness passes into light.

If only for this reason the theologian has no choice but to identify these visions as visions of God, visions of what was once manifest to faith as God the Creator, and in being forced to make that identification we are forced into the realization that even these visions are in genuine continuity with the biblical tradition or traditions. And they are so above all in actually naming or seeing a purely transcendent power, a power thereby revealed in its immediate and actual presence, and no less so in its overwhelming and total presence. Yes, we may and must identify this as an anonymous power and presence. At no point does it even hint of the presence of God as God, or of God as Word or Wisdom or "I." Nevertheless, no simple or literal anonymity is present here, and cannot be so present if only because we recognize our own ground and source in such vision, and demonstrably recognize it in the very intensity and immediacy of our response. Only bad faith could refuse or evade such a vision as a vision in some sense of God, even if not of a uniquely singular and personal God. If we can but realize that not only a total vision but also a vision of totality is at least potentially present in modern art, then we can realize that it will by necessity break through and transcend all singular and individual forms and images, including our given and historical images of God. Thus anonymity need not be a literally nameless and faceless identity, it may well promise a new and total identity, and certainly so if we can actually see our anonymity.

As Kafka has so profoundly taught us, and above all in *The Trial* and *The Castle*, we have irretrievably lost that innocence which makes possible the nonnaming of God. Theologically, what is now most difficult is to name a totally and actually anonymous presence as the image and identity of God for us. In response to this situation, the theologian is most tempted to speak of God as though God is not present in either our world or ourselves, and thus not present in our desert and abyss. This is why it has become so tempting to speak of the unknowability of God, and thereby wholly to dissociate God from the brute actuality of our world. No, our anonymity does name God, and it names God if only because it embodies a total presence, and a presence which we can not only actually see, but can see only because we can no longer see or envision what we once named as God. Just as a purely anonymous vision is impossible apart from the loss or dissolution of an interior and immanent center, so likewise is it impossible apart from the loss or reversal of a transcendent ground or center. Both of these losses, dissolutions, or reversals are present in the depths of our anonymity, and we know or realize them to be present when we discover and embody a pure immediacy in response to a totally anonymous presence. And we know or remember that this is an immediacy which once was a response to the "I" of God. That "I" has long since ceased to induce such a response, but we know a total response which is its counterpart in responding to a new and total presence, and therein we know a new presence and a new identity of what we once named as God.

Chapter Three

THE KINGDOM OF GOD

THE HISTORICAL CONFRONTATION OF OPPOSITES

Christianity is the only religion in the world which historically realized or established itself by effecting a pure negation and reversal of a visionary world. That occurred with the very birth of Christian art, for even if early Christian art is a continuation of classical and Hellenistic art it moves in the direction not simply of eroding, but actually of reversing that art. True, there is no genuine or full Christian art until Byzantine art, and Byzantine art is far more Eastern than classical, and was itself transcended and reversed in the West by the triumphant advent of Giotto. Early Christian art is striking not just because of its return to a preclassical style, but also because of its crudity and fragility, a crudity deriving not simply from a loss of clarity, but more deeply from a literalization of symbolism wherein the symbol becomes little more than a sign. After the advent of Christianity full painting and sculpture do not appear in the West for a thousand years, and therefore if only considered artistically Christianity must be identified as the most powerful counterrevolution in history. And this fact becomes of overwhelming significance when it is realized that the art which it negated was the highest and purest visual art which had until then and perhaps even thereafter been realized in the world.

The human figure first fully dawned in Greek art, a visual dawning which followed the embodiment of the birth of a full and actual human individuality in the Homeric epics. These revolutionary events may be and have been regarded both as the discovery of man and as the advent of a fully human consciousness. For the first time in history both natural and divine forms were represented and enacted as they are actually seen by the human eye, and a spatial world or cosmos was established which was grounded in a radically new and autonomous vision. Greek drama, philosophy, science, and mathematics were historical consequences of this visual revolution, a revolution which is most clearly and immediately manifest in classical sculpture. Not only do we find a pure harmony between form and content in classical sculpture, a harmony never again to be recovered, but that harmony is tangible, and it is immediately tangible, and so much so that it makes a cosmic or total equilibrium immediately and actually present. That "pure Present" which called forth Goethe's veneration is triumphantly present in fifth-century Greek sculpture, and it is totally present, a presence which in the Parthenon embodies a cosmos of energy in a purely plastic form. The victory of Christianity in the ancient world shattered this pure vision, a vision never again to be resurrected, and therewith perished a unique and organic continuum between the human, the cosmic, and the divine, a continuum that was to be succeeded by the violent dichotomies of a Christian and Western consciousness and society.

The advent of Christianity and its incredibly rapid movement into the Hellenistic world made possible for the only time in history an immediate encounter between two polar forms of consciousness. True, the original power of a purely oral eschatological language and consciousness had been diluted and transformed by the embodiment of Word in cultus and text. But Christianity initially entered the Hellenistic world before the birth of Christian texts and almost certainly with a minimal cultus that was subordinate to kerygmatic proclamation and celebration. If it was Paul and not Jesus who was the founder of a universal or catholic Christianity, this occurred by way of the establishment of a new eschatological faith and life that could be celebrated and lived in the very context of a universal society and culture. All too significantly, the advent of Pauline Christianity historically coincides with the birth of Mahayana Buddhism, for it is only in catholic or universal Christianity and Mahayana Buddhism that we may discover forms of faith or vision that are historically destined to enter and transform every form of consciousness and culture which they encounter. However, in its genesis Mahayana Buddhism did not encounter a polar opposite, and it is noteworthy that the earliest Indian art known to us is Buddhist art. Christianity and Christianity alone became a universal religion only by way of a total and violent confrontation.

Unlike Islam, which was born in a world in which the established centers of power were withering away, Christianity was born at the very moment when the classical world had realized its greatest power, at least its greatest political and social power, and at this very time Roman law and literature were creating for the first time in history a distinction be tween the public and the private realms which made possible a truly new form of individual consciousness and identity. It was not for nothing that Roman power was so forcefully directed against both Jews and Christians, but it was the Christians and not the Jews or even the Persians who posed the one mortal threat to the Roman Empire. While the miracle of the Jews may well be or have become survival itself, the miracle of Christianity is that it triumphed not only over the greatest empire in history, but also over the most power- ful culture and society which until then had existed. Yet it did not so triumph apart from a violent confrontation, a con- frontation transforming both Christianity and the classical world, and a confrontation both ending and creating an ecumenic age, the one embodying the full flowering of the ancient world, and the other inaugurating a history culmi- nating with the rise of modernity. Never before or since has such a violent historical confrontation and crisis occurred, for this is the only time in history that there is a full coming together not only of opposing, but of opposite forms of con- sciousness and identity.

Who could have foreseen that the voice of an isolated prophet would bring an end to the ancient world? If we can- not now recover the *ipsissma verba* of that voice, we are nevertheless gaining an ever increasing realization of its *ip- sissma vox*, a voice that simultaneously renews and resurrects an ancient prophetic voice even while fully actualizing a revolutionary and total identity of voice. Throughout the history of Israel the prophets and their disciples had conducted violent assaults not only upon the religion of the ancient world, but also upon all established culture and society. Here is a purely negative power in its most naked and immediate form, and it is a power which realizes itself wholly through voice, and does so even when that voice manifests itself in symbolic acts and associations. And that power was most profoundly directed against Israel itself, or against its deepest assurance and hope, so that, with Amos, the longed for and even messianic Day of the Lord became identified as a day of total darkness and destruction. No authentic prophetic oracle gives hope that this destruction can be averted, for prophetic hope before the Exile was confined to the hope in a survival of a faithful remnant. True prophetic hope is the very opposite of messianic expectation, for messianic expectation, which has occurred and does occur throughout the world, is a longing for the total historical triumph of an existing political or imperial power. Prophetic hope, on the contrary, is directed to the end or dissolution of all historical or manifest power and identity.

The justice for which the prophets called is not to be confused with historical or legal justice, just as the act of repent-once or turning which they demanded is not to be understood as a return to a covenantal community. Even as breakthroughs from the archaic world were occurring at this very time in Greece and India, and breakthroughs initially realizing truly individual forms and identities of consciousness, so, too, all of the canonical prophets called for a totally individual act of faith, an act demanding an exile from the previous form and identity of Israel. The prophetic oracles are long distant from a Deuteronomic sense of a sacred people and its world historical destiny, just as they are equally distant from the world of Torah and cultus. Here, an overwhelmingly negative power is directed against every form of self-identity which is grounded in either sacred history or sacred space, and so much so that the radical hope which the prophetic oracle offers can have no possible historical or spatial meaning. Hence the pre-Exilic and antipriestly prophetic voice is a purely negative voice, and even its post-Exilic and priestly expressions continue to revolve about a pure act of negation. And it is just this act of negation which realizes a truly new form and identity of faith.

When the prophetic voice is renewed and reborn in Jesus, it seemingly has a very different form. No longer are there assaults upon historical and spatial identity, and no longer is there any kind of call for justice, or any historical hope at all. The imagery, movement, and rhythm of the prophetic oracles embody a marvelous power, and again and again they give compelling witness to the presence of a particular and individual voice. No such power or witness is present in the *logia* of the synoptic Gospels, and it is all too clear that one is here confronting an anonymous voice. And not only an anonymous voice, but a naked and faceless voice, a voice freed of every spatial source and horizon. Not only can one not associate such a voice with a spatial point or horizon, but its very presence negates horizon as such, embodying a presence that is totally present here and now. Here, then, voice as voice is present and immediately present in its most total form and identity. This is a total presence of voice which can realize itself only by dissolving every other form of presence. Consequently, its very identity as a totality of voice brings an end to all identity which is not present in voice, and does so in such a way as to erase the very possibility of such presence.

THE MYSTERY OF THE KINGDOM OF GOD

The victory of Christianity over the ancient or pagan world brought an end to the highest culture which until then had existed in the West, and the only culture which the world has ever known in which cosmos and consciousness stand forth in their own distinct identities even while remaining in an integral and unified relationship with each other. The iconoclastic shattering of ancient art and literature gives us some sense of this catastrophe, and the emasculation of Greek philosophy in Christian scholasticism gives us another, to say nothing of the literal end of classical science and mathematics in the medieval Christian world. Without doubt the end of the world, the end of a fully human and cultural world, was realized in the triumph of Christianity. Yet it is also true that Christianity vanquished the ancient and classical world only by ceasing to be itself. This truth becomes decisively apparent upon realizing that when Christian understanding reaches its patristic maturity in Augustine the proclamation of Jesus has become so transformed as to be unrecognizable. Augustine's *City of God* marks the historical point at which a Western Christian understanding of God has realized itself only by annulling its original ground. And this Western Christian transformation of the gospel remained normative for another fifteen hundred years, as witness the fact that the modern historical discovery of the eschatological identity of Jesus came as a cataclysmic shock to the Christian world.

While it is true that an apocalyptic faith was reborn again

and again in the radical expressions of Christian sectarianism and Christian mysticism, and that a rebirth of apocalyptic imagery occurred in medieval sculpture and painting, and perhaps also in medieval architecture and Dante, it is also true that a comprehensive rebirth of the apocalyptic in European romanticism and in nineteenth-century radical political and idealistic philosophy remained invisible as such to the believing world of Christian faith. The truth is that it was only with and in the end of Christendom that the original proclamation of Jesus was fully reborn in language and consciousness and that this rebirth occurred by way of a violent assault upon both Christian transcendence and the Christian God. No more profound assault upon Christian transcendence has ever been conducted than that which is present in the modern historical consciousness, and this consciousness initially realized itself by discovering the ancient world or worlds, thereby discovering a new world of the Bible. It has yet to be demonstrated that this new world of the Bible can be reconciled with any existing form of Christianity, and it is noteworthy that to this day modern Christianity has not yet evolved a theology which is biblical and systematic at once. But what is most striking is that the attempt has not even been made, or not openly made, to evolve a new theology which is grounded in the proclamation of Jesus.

Even New Testament scholars have refused to take up the task of seeking theological meaning in the eschatological language of Jesus, perhaps because of their deep historical realization that an ancient language can have no possible theological meaning for us. Or, at least, it can have little or no meaning in terms of our inherited theological language and categories. Yet the eschatological language of Jesus was reborn in the nineteenth century, and reborn in such a way as to become a primal foundation of true modernity. For example, Heidegger, in commenting upon the Introduction to Hegel's *Phenomenology of Spirit*, can say that experience is for Hegel the "subjectness of the absolute subject," is the *"parousia* of the Absolute." Such language is meaningful to the philosopher today, but it is not meaningful to the theologian, and this despite the fact that *parousia* or final and total presence lies at the very center of the original language of Christianity. Total and final presence is a leitmotif of modern art, as we have seen, and so likewise of modern literature. And it is so only by way of the actuality in consciousness and experience of a total presence, a presence shattering every individual center of identity. Such a total shattering first occurs in the original language of Jesus. And only a reversal of this primal shattering made possible the contruction of the Western Christian identity of God.

There is no deeper mystery in the modern Christian world than the identity of the Kingdom of God. If only for this reason the language of Jesus is alien to us, and most deeply alien at just those points where we are most deeply affected by our given identity of God. Above all it is the purely transcendent identity of God, an identity more powerfully present today than ever previously in the West, which is the most pervasive veil for us of the New Testament symbol of the Kingdom of God. Now it is of fundamental historical significance that the language of the Kingdom of God occurs in no prophet prior to Jesus, at least so far as we know. True, it is present in the proclamation of John the Baptist, but we know this only through the Gospels, and for the Gospels John the Baptist is simply the precursor of Jesus. We also find something like its counterpart in the Dead Sea Scriptures, but no straightforward or open language of the Kingdom of God. It is also of equal historical significance that the language of the Kingdom of God dominates the language of Paul, whether directly or indirectly, and then it progressively disappears from the language of the New Testament, until it is virtually absent from the Gospel of John. Historically, Jesus is the center of this eschatological language, and whether we move toward the Torah or toward the Catholic church, that language ever more decisively disappears. Indeed, with the establishment of Christianity as the officical religion of the Roman Empire this eschatological language came to an initial end.

Now we have every reason to believe that Jesus was the first prophet to announce the actual presence of the Kingdom of God in any sense. It could even be said that it is precisely here that the uniqueness of his proclamation lies, for there is nothing that more distinguishes this identity of the Kingdom of God than its actual presence. Of course, this is not a simple presence, as witness the fact that the Kingdom is also future. Nevertheless, the actuality of its presence, in whatever sense, wholly distinguishes an eschatological Kingdom of God from a prophetic Day of the Lord, just as it distinguishes it from any mythical form of an apocalyptic Kingdom of God. Moreover, presence here is *parousia* or total presence, and it is just for this reason that we have long since come to understand it as an eschatological presence. But it cannot be a total or final or eschatological presence unless it is the presence of the fullness of God, a presence which by necessity must affect what faith apprehends as the pure transcendence of God. The strongest opponents of Jesus were the most deeply devout, and this includes not only the scribes and the Pharisees, but also Jesus' disciples and, at the end, most deeply those disciples. Just as messianic expectations of any sort turned Jesus' hearers away from him, so it is that a confident faith in God is a profound barrier to eschatological faith, and perhaps the deepest barrier that was present to his hearers. For it is precisely faith in the transcendent God which most diverts attention from the actual presence of the Kingdom.

As New Testament and patristic language evolved further and further away from eschatological language, it did so above all in its understanding of God or Spirit, and most particularly so insofar as it understood Spirit or God as the One who is simply other than cosmos or world. Thereby and therein there can be no integral relation between God and the world, and therefore no possibility of an actual presence of God in the world, and thus no eschatological presence. Then Kingdom of God literally becomes Kingdom of Heaven, as is true in early Christian art, and the City of God becomes not only essentially but also literally other than the city of man. It was Augustine, and not Luther, who created a two-kingdom theology, even if he only brought to its full resolution a movement of faith and belief which had been evolving for almost four hundred years. But it is this ultimate distinction between two kingdoms which was the first full theoretical expression of that dualism which soon came to dominate and overwhelm the West. Nothing could more foreclose the possibility of understanding a total presence, and a total presence of God in world; and not only of understanding a total or eschatological presence but also of envisioning or speaking such a presence. Of course, this is not the only ground of Western or Augustinian theology, as witness

Augustine's understanding of God as the ground and center of consciousness, an understanding which made possible his revolutionary realization of a fully personal and individual form and identity of consciousness. Yet that realization was itself destined to evolve a form of self-consciousness which moved further and further away from any possible positive ground in cosmos or world.

Perhaps what is most difficult to apprehend in eschatological language is its simultaneous affirmation and negation of world. The Kingdom of God is fully present, yes, but its presence effects a full negation of everything which otherwise stands forth as world. The presence of the Kingdom of God is simultaneously salvation and judgment, and its fullness as salvation is inseparable from its fullness as judgment, so that the redemption of the world is simultaneously the end of the world. A full parallel to this dialectical equivalence of total affirmation and total negation is present in Mahayana Buddhism, but while it became normative in Buddhism, it became invisible and subterranean in Christianity, and so much so that when it was resurrected in the modern world it became manifest as a violent assault upon both Christianity and the Christian God. For it is the God who alone is God, the purely transcendent God, who is most distant from an eschatological presence. No such God is present in Jesus, or not in the eschatological and parabolic language of Jesus, and cannot be so present if only because that language celebrates and embodies a total presence of God. Only a dualistic consciousness would necessarily be impelled to understand a total presence of God as a pantheistic deification of world. But that is just the form of consciousness that ever more decisively evolved in the West, hence the profound resistance of the Western Christian to the very possibility of a divine and total presence.

Yet we must also come to see that there can be no real *parousia* of God, no real final and total presence of God, apart from a negation of every other presence and identity of God. This is just the kind of negation which occurs in modern apocalyptic language and understanding, as witness Blake and Hegel, just as it also occurs in Paul's negation of the Law, and in the ancient prophets' negation of the old Israel. The very identity of Jesus as a prophet can only mean that a comparable negation was present in him, and otherwise it is virtually impossible to account for the profound hostility which his proclamation aroused. That offense which Paul so deeply discovered in an eschatological Word, an offense reenacted by Luther, Kierkegaard, and Dostoevski, is not simply an offense induced by human self-righteousness, else it would not be so deep; it is far rather an offense induced by a negation of God, by a negation of every identity of God which stands apart from an eschatological presence. But that means a negation of every identity of God which is present to consciousness as God, or which stands out or apart from consciousness, or which is manifest as God and God alone. This is the God who is manifest in what the Christian alone knows as the Law, a Law from which a redemptive presence of God is absent, and absent because of the presence of God in an eschatological presence.

THE KINGDOM OF GOD BEYOND GOD

"We pray to God," Meister Eckhart says, "to be free from God." Such a radical mystical call to full redemption is in full continuity with the original proclamation of Christianity. The God whom Jesus addressed as *Abba* is present as God only through the absence of the God of pure transcendence. Such a presence is itself an eschatological event, for to know God as *Abba* is to know a full and final revelation. But that revelation can be present, or can fully and finally be present, only by negating and transcending the revelation which it fulfills and completes. It is precisely a bondage to former revelation, or to preeschatological epiphanies of God, which is the deepest barrier to an acceptance of the actual presence of the Kingdom of God. At this point even the Gospel of John may be judged to be an eschatological Gospel, for it goes far beyond Paul by virtually identifying the God of the old covenant as Satan. The Jesus of the Fourth Gospel can affirm that the descendants of Abraham are children of the Devil because they do not believe the truth he tells them, and they do not believe because they do not know God, the God who is Spirit and Spirit alone. Quite clearly such a Spirit is truly other than the God of the old covenant and the old revelation, and is so just because it is fully and finally present.

Only within the context of an eschatological movement of faith, a movement from darkness to Light or from flesh to Spirit, is it possible to apprehend the decisive significance of an eschatological now. An eschatological now is a total moment because it embodies a total presence, a presence immediately and actually released by an ultimate and final event. When the Gospel of Luke reports that Jesus saw Satan fall like lightning from heaven, it is clearly recording the occurrence of just such an event. Only as a consequence of such an ultimate event is the Kingdom of God at hand, and we may well surmise that apart from such an event it is not even possible to speak of the Kingdom of God. Otherwise why is the Kingdom of God as such absent from the Old Testament? But this can only mean that the God who is manifest or nameable apart from an eschatological event or presence cannot be the God who is nameable or manifest in an eschatological Spirit, Light, or Word. And from the point of view of eschatological Light, that God can only be the God of darkness or Satan. Hell, demons, and Satan are New Testament and not Old Testament motifs, and nothing is more primary in the Gospel narratives than the conflict of Jesus with Satan and the demons. Indeed, in the Gospels it is only the demons and Satan who immediately know the ultimate identity of Jesus. And that is an identity which is not simply directed against darkness, but which realizes itself in its negation of darkness.

Of course, the God who is manifest in an eschatological Word is the God of the Old Testament. It is God the Creator, God the giver of Torah, and God the Redeemer of Israel, who is present in the Kingdom of God. But God is nameable by none of these names when manifest in and as an eschatological presence. And to understand or envision the Kingdom of God by way of these former names of God is to refuse an eschatological presence, and to refuse it by clinging to a pre-incarnate identity of God, an identity which by necessity is other than a final and ultimate identity. So it is that in an eschatological situation a partial identity of God can become a demonic identity of God, and a preincarnate God can be identified as Satan. Nor is such an identification confined to the ancient world; we find its full parallel in the modern, as in Blake's naming of the Christian God as Satan, or in Hegel's understanding of the given and manifest God as the "false

infinite" or abstract Spirit, or in Melville's naming of Moby
Dick. By no means does such an eschatological naming mean
that God simply is Satan, but rather that the fullness and finality of God's presence negates all previous presences and
identities of God, and those identities and presences then become dark and demonic because they divert attention from
an ultimate presence, and thus oppose the actuality of that
presence. The demons with which Jesus battled are the demons of faith, and they are above all present in that faith
which says God rather than *Abba* in response to the advent of
the Kingdom of God.

Only in an eschatological situation, or in an eschatological
movement of faith, does the identity of God as God become a
negation of faith. To name God as God is to name the transcendent God, the God who is Creator and Lord, the God
who is envisioned as being above and before. This is above all
the God who cannot be totally present, and cannot be finally
present, for to be finally and totally present would be to cease
to be before and above. Moreover, it is the transcendent
identity of God which realizes itself in consciousness as the
God who is beyond, who is wholly other, and wholly other
and beyond every possible form or identity of consciousness.
Here, the transcendent God of the Bible is the full and exact
contrary of the Homeric gods. Those gods, which themselves
are the products of one of the greatest revolutions in history,
and a revolution historically coincident with the prophetic
revolution, are gods making manifest a wholly immanent
presence, and a presence of divinity in a fully human form, a
form which actually can be seen, and seen by a vision both
released by and embodied in the Homeric poems. Nevertheless, these gods are wholly other than men, and are so above
all by virtue of their immortal state, a state which is not only

denied humanity, but a state which in the Homeric or Apollonian tradition is the very antithesis of human identity. An Olympian heaven is a heaven in which there can be no human presence, even if it is also that heaven which releases the fullest vision or standing forth of consciousness.

Even though Greek vision knows a fully immanent presence, it does not know a total presence, and cannot know a total presence if only because it ever remains grounded in a source or ground lying outside of consciousness. That ground disappears in total presence, and must disappear to make possible a total presence, and so long as it remains there can be no possibility of an eschatological presence. Therefore, both classical vision and biblical transcendence are equally antithetical to eschatological faith, and equally opposed to an eschatological presence, and all too naturally Christianity historically realized itself by an attempted destruction of both the classical and the Jewish worlds. That battle continues even to the present day, but just as a classical world was resurrected in Christendom, so likewise was Judaism resurrected in the Church, and perhaps for that very reason both the Church and Christendom have always existed in a negative relationship to eschatological vision and faith. Indeed, the historical evolution of both the Church and Christendom continually carried each further and further away from an eschatological ground, a process challenged only by eschatological or apocalyptic forces which arose again and again to challenge the dominant movements of Christendom and the Church. Christendom came to an end with the dawn of modernity, and the Church progressively regressed to a sectarian identity, but a new apocalypticism burst forth with a revolutionary fury, and in identities both demonic and divine, both pathological and free.

Chapter Four

HISTORY
AND
ESCHATOLOGY

The rebirth of apocalypticism in medieval Europe initiated or gave expression to a historical process that was to
culminate with the social, political, and cultural revolutions
of the modern world. Medieval apocalypticism hurled itself
against both Church and State, finding in each an inherent
opposite of the Kingdom of God which it expected, and re-
joicing in the advent of a new time which would bring all
history to an end. What is most distinctive about this new
movement is its apprehension of an absolute antithesis between the totality of history and the Kingdom of God, an antithesis transforming an established dualism between God
and the world into a truly new apprehension of a purely
negative relationship between history and transcendence.
This apocalypticism was born at the very time that a new
sense and identity of transcendence was dawning in the West,
a pure transcendence that was nevertheless expressible in

visual symbolism and conceptual thinking, as witness the triumphs in this period of Gothic architecture and scholastic theology. Dante's *Comedy* both embodies this transcendence and integrally and systematically relates it to both the macrocosm and the microcosm of history. A new humanism was born in this period, a humanism revolving about the birth of an autonomous subject of consciousness, and a humanism struggling against the objective feudal and monarchic grounds of both Church and State.

Here lies the ground of a distinctively Western movement of modern history. On the one hand, a new transcendent Subject, a fully transcendent Subject, yes, but also a Subject that can be embodied in vision, thinking, and language. On the other hand, a new immanent subject, a subject that ever more gradually becomes the center of its own world, and not only the center but also the primary actor in that world. Nothing like this was previously present in history, for the classical world had never known either a purely transcendent Subject or a self-conscious center or subject, just as it had never known a true gulf or chasm between the subject and the object of consciousness. While that gulf was initially established by Israel, and thence burst forth in the Hellenistic world, it is not until the coming of the Gothic age in Europe that we may discover a form of consciousness that is grounded in a tension or opposition between an immanent center of consciousness and its transcendent ground or source. A vibrant and violent energy underlies medieval sculpture and architecture, an energy not to be found in the classical world, and unlike its classical counterparts in Euripides and Hellenistic sculpture, it threatens to break out of all artistic form. The classical consciousness knew a finite and bounded cosmos, a cosmos limited by but also grounded in a celestial transcendence. But with the dawn of modern science, the seeds of which are already present in Gothic Europe, the cosmos of the ancient world comes to an end, and in that ending there disappears every real distinction between the heavens and the earth, and the real world is no longer envisioned and conceived as a finite and hierarchically ordered whole, but rather as an open and infinite universe which is united only by the identity of its mathematical laws.

Underlying this new and violent energy of consciousness is a purely negative relationship between its poles, a relationship which does not simply integrally relate the subject of consciousness to its ground, but which realizes that relationship by way of a profound opposition or tension between a progressively immanent and solitary self-consciousness and the totality of its ground. That tension finally exploded throughout all of Europe, and it exploded in all the domains of society and consciousness, so that for the first time in history there occurred a total transformation of consciousness and society in a single even if comprehensive historical movement. While this movement has not yet reached its full consummation, its ground has certainly and irreversibly been established, and in the twentieth century it realized both a global and a mass embodiment. Throughout this movement there is a continual flow and counterflow of turbulent energy, and while it can be captured in a moment of calm as in Mozart and Cézanne, that calm inevitably proves to be an all too temporary and precarious fusion of discordant opposites or contraries. The sheer violence of pure negativity underlies this revolutionary process, a violence which finally can neither be stilled nor assuaged.

The uniquely Western and Christian identity of this pure negativity can be apprehended by noting the difference between the negative movement of Greek tragedy and its counterpart in modern tragedy. Destiny is the real problem of Greek tragedy, a destiny that is always directed against the full *areté* or uniquely human power of the hero, and which is the inevitable fate into which the gods lead humanity. But the defeat and destruction of the Greek tragic hero is a dramatic and interior reenactment of the cultic death and resurrection of Dionysus, and most if not all of the Greek tragedies culminate in a reconciliation of humanity with the gods. While the tragic hero dares to cross the boundary between humanity and the gods, and becomes truly heroic precisely in crossing that boundary, his or her inevitable immolation effects a real purgation of a human world which is necessarily blighted by the very presence of a divine or sacred power. No such reconciliation is present in the mature tragedies of Shakespeare and Racine, except when tragedy transcends itself in *The Tempest*, and in modern tragedy the action or movement of destiny most fully realizes itself by becoming wholly internalized in self-consciousness. But this self-consciousness is a divided and doubled consciousness, a consciousness which is alienated from itself, and which realizes its very life and power by assaulting and negating itself. The modern tragic hero is in most profound conflict with his own most intimate and interior ground, and the culmination of the tragedy is not a sacrificial immolation but rather the brutal and ultimate event of death, as for the first time the full human act of death becomes the source not of reconciliation, but of a total affirmation.

There is no harmony or coinherence of contrary or opposite powers in either Greek or modern tragedy, for tragic action or movement always shatters harmony or coinherence. But a broken harmony is healed or assuaged by the movement of Greek tragedy, whereas the movement of modern tragedy deepens the tragic discord, and realizes or fulfills itself by bringing an end to the very possibility of harmony or peace, or, at least, an end to the possibility of an interior peace and calm. The violent energy released by modern tragedy never comes to an end, for it is carried forward by the spectator or reader, and it inevitably has a revolutionary effect upon its social and historical world. While Shakespeare and Racine may not have immediately led to the English and French Revolutions, they embodied and released a total energy which soon found its own political expression. In this perspective we can identify Rembrandt as a tragic painter, for his portraits and self-portraits again and again give expression to a vibrant center of self-consciousness which leaps out of the canvas into an infinite and open universe in which there are neither boundaries nor walls. Throughout this world of revolutionary modernity a purely negative energy is realized and released in a wholly immanent and immediate identity. And it is a purely negative energy, an energy that embodies itself by negating itself, by negating its innermost center and source. Therefore it is an apocalyptic energy, an energy embodying a total presence, and embodying that presence by way of a real and actual negation of any other identity or presence.

What is most distinctive and unique about modern revolution is that it effects a real negation of its initial and original ground only to realize and embody that ground itself in a new and comprehensive process and identity. This process is a continual and forward-moving process, even if it undergoes multiple and violently conflicting expressions, and even if it proceeds in both revolutionary and counterrevolutionary directions. Modern revolution embodies itself in a comprehensive transformation of both consciousness and society, and that transformation moves irresistibly and irreversibly to ever more comprehensive expressions, as a total presence realizes and embodies itself in an ever fuller and more comprehensively total identity. True, it proceeds out of ancient revolutions which occurred in both Greece and Israel, but not only does it merge and unite the grounds of those revolutions, but it also embodies them in a new and potentially universal history, a history realizing a universal transformation of consciousness and society. Modern revolutionary history is apocalyptic insofar as it revolves about a forward movement of radical and total negation, a negation realizing a total presence, but it is a new apocalypse insofar as it embodies that presence in the actuality of history and in the fullness of consciousness.

Revelation and Revolution

How is revelation to be identified and conceived? There are multiple forms of revelation throughout the world, and so much so that it is impossible to arrive at a common identity of revelation. Until the Koran, however, if even then, revelation is never text, or never initially or originally a text. While revelation may come to be identified as text, this is always the consequence of a long historical development, with the exception of the Christian canonization of the New Testament. Perhaps the very rapidity with which the New Testament was canonized has induced Christians to confine revelation to the text of the Bible. Yet both Catholicism and Judaism have always understood revelation through tradition, just as have all other religious traditions in the world, and the truth is that Protestantism has done likewise, for each form of Protestantism apprehends revelation through its own particular tradition. Accordingly, *sola scriptura* is an illusion, or an illusion when it is understood literally, for an unmediated and disembodied Scripture simply doesn't exist. And Christians of any kind can only identify revelation with the text of Scripture by giving a comparable even if disguised authority to an ecclesiastical tradition and community.

From the very beginning Christians have understood revelation to be an evolving and forward-moving process, from Genesis to Apocalypse, and from the Old Testament and the Old Israel to the New. The real problem arises when the "new" is simply identified with the New Testament. Nietzsche remarked that the greatest sin on the Western conscience was its joining of the Old and New Testaments, and certainly from a literary point of view the New Testament is inferior to the Old Testament, and for the most part vastly inferior. The Greek of the New Testament is not only a simple Greek, but also a common or vulgar Greek, a Greek that was employed by originally non-Greek-speaking peoples. Virtually all Christians know the New Testament, and fundamentally and deeply know the New Testament, through a language vastly removed from the original, and not simply because they read it in a language different from Greek, but rather because they know it in a language worlds removed from the common Greek of the New Testament text. And whether this be a liturgical language or the exalted language of Luther's translation or the King James Version or their counterparts, it is nevertheless a language which historically is far distant from the original. So one can only respond ironically to any Christian belief in the finality of the Bible or the New Testament. It is doubtful if it is possible for anyone to believe that the Bible is literally revelation, and we must not forget that the actual original texts of the Bible are unknown to us, and there could not have been an original singular text in any case. So what can it mean to say that the text of the Bible is literally inspired?

What we can speak of is the impact of the biblical revelation upon history, and not simply upon the history of the churches or the Church, but rather upon the very fullness of history. This is the problem which the modern theologian has abandoned, and abandoned in large part because, since the French Revolution, Christendom has withered away and the churches have ceased to be of fundamental historical importance, and thus there simply is no way of associating the fullness of history with any form of ecclesiastical Christianity. Of course, Hegel created the philosophy of history by understanding the whole of postclassical Western history as the historical realization of the Incarnation, but this is possible only by way of a negation and transcendence of ecclesiastical Christianity. But all modern philosophies of history are Hegelian, for even when they attempt a reversal of Hegelianism — as did Marx, Burckhardt, and Nietzsche — they continue to maintain a Hegelian conception of history and a Hegelian language, even if in reverse form. What we have certainly not had in the modern world is a non-Hegelian theology of history, except in those innumerable theologies which have regressed to a premodern form. Nevertheless, we have been given a remarkable number of theological studies of history, all written in total indifference to the Church.

Once revelation is dissociated from a simple and unilateral relationship with the Church, or with any ecclesiastical community or communities, then it becomes possible to understand revelation as existing in a comprehensive relationship with the fullness of history, and therefore with the full actuality of society and consciousness. We have long since learned that the New Testament reflects and embodies a wide variety of differing and conflicting communities and beliefs, just as we have learned that patristic Christianity must historically be understood as embracing both Catholic and "heretical" Christianity, and it is by no means clear that the former is in fuller continuity with primitive Christianity, or even in fuller or more organic continuity with later Western history. Certainly medieval apocalyptic Christianity is far closer to earlier heretical groups such as the Montanists than it is to Catholic Christianity, just as medieval mysticism is at least as close to Gnostic Christianity as it is to the Catholic church. So, likewise, the revolution which burst forth in Gothic Europe transcended all forms of ancient Christianity and ushered in a truly new world. Even if Gothic civilization grew out of Romanesque civilization, which itself was an extension of Carolingian culture, it is nevertheless true that something fundamentally new is at hand in the Gothic world, as can clearly be seen both in St. Francis and Giotto, to say nothing of the theological revolution effected by Albert the Great and Thomas Aquinas. This new world cannot be understood simply by way of its continuity with ancient Christianity, and this is clearly so because of the manifest continuity between Gothic Europe and the Renaissance and Reformation.

Dante's *Comedy* gives us clear and decisive evidence for the presence of a form of vision and consciousness in the Gothic world which is simultaneously in organic continuity with both ancient and biblical Christianity and with the fullness of both the Reformation and the Renaissance. Obviously the Bible and the whole Bible is an essential and fundamental ground of the *Comedy*, but so likewise is it obvious that the *Comedy* fully anticipates the revolutionary European world of the sixteenth and seventeenth centuries. While it is true that the *Comedy* is grounded in a Ptolemaic and classical world view, it is also true that a new and violent energy is present in the *Comedy*, and above all in its new and even complementary visions of both man and God. Unlike a classical celestial transcendence, in the *Paradisio* heaven is a radiant eternal light which is the source of a love dispersed throughout the universe, a love that moves the celestial bodies, and a love that finally reveals itself in a strange vision of a circling "face." Only Gothic vision fully unveils the "face" of God, a face that was progressively humanized in the development of Romanesque and Gothic art, and a face that will not be fully realized until Michelangelo. Throughout this process transcendence becomes progressively manifest as transcendent love, and a purely transcendent God ever more fully and more finally becomes manifest in and as the immanent face of Christ.

In the sculpture of Michelangelo a divine and transcendent energy becomes fully embodied in a plastic and immediate presence, a total presence finally transcending and exploding all possible form, so that recent criticism has identified Michelangelo as a Baroque artist. Therein the late Michelangelo is truly a historical contemporary of the late

Shakespeare, and therewith each is a historical parallel to the new mathematical physics, a physics that in the twentieth century destroys the very possibility of visualization. But this new and total energy, an energy human, cosmic, and divine, pulses at the very center of a comprehensive historical movement, a revolutionary movement embodying both the real end of the ancient world and the real beginning of a new and universal historical world. Both that end and that beginning are eschatological or apocalyptic, indeed, the very coincidence of beginning and end can only be apocalyptic, and most clearly apocalyptic insofar as each is an irresistible and irreversible movement or act. The force and finality of this movement are fully present in modern music, the most revolutionary of all the European art forms, and here we may actually and immediately hear a total presence. At no other point is the distance between Europe and Asia so great as in the domain of music, and the mere fact that we can hear some continuity between Gregorian chant and Baroque music is a decisive sign of a biblical presence in modern revolution.

Even the most reactionary of modern theologians, although also perhaps the greatest, Karl Barth, could hear in Mozart the intonation of a biblical heaven, possibly because it is only in Mozart among the great composers that there is no presence of an alien transcendence. Even in the unfinished Requiem there is an absence of a truly numinous awe, which leads us to realize that in Mozart both the sacred and the profane are absent, and so likewise is absent any identity which stands out from its opposite or contrary. Immanence and transcendence are here united, and so likewise are heaven and earth and God and man. We may suspect that there is a comparable coincidence present in Chinese music, as there appears to be in Chinese landscape painting, but the very monotony of Chinese as of all Asian music is worlds or universes removed from the pure harmony of Mozart. That harmony is a purely Western harmony, and although it cannot so purely be heard elsewhere, and has wholly disappeared in the twentieth century, it is anticipated and foreshadowed in Greek sculpture, even if Greek music is lost to us. But never in the ancient world is harmony so purely realized as in Mozart, and never for that matter in the European world before Mozart, which leads one to sense that the deepest harmony is possible only on the basis of the prior presence of the deepest tension and opposition. While musically, Mozart was far less revolutionary than Beethoven or Schoenberg, he nevertheless may be the most revolutionary of composers, and this because he so immediately and totally embodies a *coincidentia oppositorum*, a new and apocalyptic *coincidentia oppositorum* in which the opposites as opposites disappear.

Who is to say that the Book of Revelation is more fully revelation than is the music of Mozart? Or that it is more fully or more truly apocalyptic? We might more responsibly think that Mozart is only possible on the basis of the Book of Revelation, or on the basis of that apocalyptic faith of which it is an expression. If it is true that there is a true *coincidentia* of opposites in Mozart, then we must realize that such *coincidentia* is impossible apart from the actual and immediate presence of real opposites, a presence which we justifiably recognize as apocalyptic. True, when full *coincidentia* occurs the opposites disappear, but this is at least as true of the parabolic language of Jesus as it is of the purest music of Mozart. If we identify the former as fully eschatological or apocalylptic, then there seems to be little reason for with-holding an apocalyptic identification from the latter, and most particularly so if we are to identify Mozart as a Christian artist. But if he is a Christian artist he transcends the Bible just as Dante and Milton did before him, and not only Milton and Dante, but a whole vast and comprehensive body of modern vision. Yet here the Bible is transcended by being preserved, by being realized and released in a new conscious-ness, and a new consciousness and vision and voice which for the first time realizes and embodies biblical faith in a fully ac-tual and potentially universal history.

CULTURAL AND POLITICAL REVOLUTION

The origins of modern revolution lie thousands of years in our past, but historically we can sense that its beginning oc-curs with an original naming of Yah or Yahweh, with the epiphany of a radical and negative transcendent power among a wandering group of nomads in the ancient Near East. This epiphany eventually gave birth to Israel, Judaism, and the Old Testament, and here we may observe the advent of a people who simultaneously absorbed the higher social and cultural forms of the ancient Near East even while negat-ing and transcending their interior and human ground. Pro-phetic iconoclasm was a violent assault upon the totality of vi-sion and consciousness, and so likewise upon all of the social, political, and economic institutions of the ancient Near East, for its affirmation of Yahweh or the Lord was so total as to negate every other ground of society and consciousness. Thereby a new energy was released in the world, a violent and negative energy, and an energy directed against everything which previously had stood forth as a center of meaning and identity. While such an energy would be reborn in Islam, it was earlier reborn in apocalyptic Judaism, and out of this rebirth there issued the origins of Christianity. How long a way from the original naming of Yah to the total vision of God and the world in Dante, and yet such a baffling historical movement in fact occurred, as a raw and elemental transcendence eventually and comprehensively passed into the fullness of the imagination.

Ancient Israel was once again reborn in Calvinism, and most particularly so in radical Calvinism, and most forcefully so in seventeenth-century England and early America. Milton is the poet-prophet par excellence, the only poet since the Old Testament to totally fuse a prophetic and a poetic language, and the only poet who created an epic which was itself the embodiment of an actual and political revolution. While all genuine epics have both a political and a revolutionary ground, it is only in *Paradise Lost* that political revolution passes fully into language, as the voices of Puritans, Ranters, Levelers, and the like realize their pure and all too human power in the most exalted poetry yet given us. Cromwell's secretary was not a passive witness of revolution, he was an active participant, and most powerfully so when in the wake of political defeat he wrote *Paradise Lost*. An ancient Greek would not have been surprised to learn that a blind seer was to create the most glorious visual poetic imagery in any language, but an ancient Christian might well have been shocked, and shocked because no other religious tradition engaged in such a violent assault upon the visual world as did early Christianity. Yet no poet, not even Dante, is more Christian than Milton, and if ecclesiastical Christians cannot imagine a Christian Isaiah or Jeremiah, this does nothing to lessen or erase an overwhelmingly Christian presence and voice. And this is a Christian and revolutionary voice, and a voice, indeed, that is Christian only by way of its revolutionary power and identity.

The Blake who could believe that the history of repression is written in *Paradise Lost*, and that Milton's Christ is the "Governor" or "Reason" of repression, could also note "The reason Milton wrote in fetters when he wrote of Angels & God, and at liberty when he wrote of Devils & Hell, is because he was a true Poet and of the Devil's party without knowing it." This early Blake could know Satan as the fire of political revolution, but the late Blake identified Satan as God the Creator and Judge, and first did so poetically when he reenacted and reversed *Paradise Lost* in his first apocalyptic epic, *Milton*. Then, in *Jerusalem*, Blake realized the apocalyptic identity of Satan as Christ, and of Milton's Satan as Christ, that revolutionary Satan whom Robert Lowell at the very end of his life could name as *Christus Liberator* or the hermetic God. Certainly Satan is the poetic and dramatic center of *Paradise Lost*, and as opposed to the totally passive figure who is encrusted in ice in the *Inferno*, Milton's Satan is the pure embodiment of a total and negative energy, and an energy that is the ruling power of a fallen history and a fallen cosmos. This apocalyptic identification of Satan as the Lord of an inverted cosmos not only calls forth the fullness of poetic language in its most majestic power, but in that very language there is embodied a radical historical actualization which establishes history itself as the sole arena of a total and cosmic destiny.

Both classical and biblical epic are reenacted in *Paradise*

Lost, and just as Milton believed that he was possessed by Moses, so likewise did he reenact in a new and Christian epic the ancient epics of Homer and Vergil. But whereas classical and biblical epics are epics of ascent, or epics of fall and ascent which culminate in victory, the action of *Paradise Lost* revolves about the downward movement of fall, and the Christian epic culminates with the expulsion of Adam and Eve from paradise. Sin and death, or original sin and original death, are the real subject of *Paradise Lost*, as the epic moves from their potential ground to their final realization. It is as though hell were the sole subject of Dante's *Comedy*, for here is a Calvinist mind which is greater than Calvin's, and a scholastic doctor who reverses the doctors and fathers of the Church. Even though Milton involuntarily wrote a parody of *Paradise Lost* in *Paradise Regained*, the ultimate power of the former is thereby only reinforced, and made yet further manifest as an eschatological power, a power effecting an irreversible end of a former world, and not only the end of an earlier human world, but the end of a pure and unfallen transcendence as well. It is not only the ground of human monarchy which perishes in *Paradise Lost*, but also the established ground of divine monarchy, as the power of the Creator is now most fully present in the face and voice of Satan, a voice and a face which are now apocalyptically revealed as the originating center of a pure and negative energy.

That energy is a violent energy, perhaps the most violent poetic energy which has ever been released, and its deepest violence is most fully manifest in the very exaltation of Milton's imagery. All the dazzling power of Dante's paradise is now manifest in Satan, and Blake in redrawing Dante's paradise as hell was thereby fulfilling an authentically Miltonic movement. Yet it is precisely when all transcendent power is manifest and visible as centering in Satan, that heaven is finally closed to all human vision and entry, and earth or history alone becomes a final and a total destiny. Both the epic and the tragic heroes of the ancient world anticipated that destiny, but the classical world was innocent of pure evil or Satan, and hence could not envision a sin and death that are final and ultimate. Therefore they were closed to the vision of a final expulsion from paradise, just as they were closed to the possibility of the finality of history, a possibility which becomes actuality in *Paradise Lost*. And that is just the actuality which appeared in the English Revolution, an apocalyptic revolution which was not only directed against monarchy but also against every power and authority which cannot be embodied in the human mind and voice. And the English Revolution, unlike all previous political revolutions, proved to be an irresistible and irreversible historical force.

Twenty years after the publication of *Paradise Lost* Newton gave the world his *Principia*. A theological mind might identify this work as the authentic *Paradise Regained*, for the Newton who banished hypotheses from "experimental philosophy" was the Newton who was the fullest embodiment of the scientific revolution of the seventeenth century, a revolution which destroyed a transcendent celestial world by an ontological and mathematical realization of an infinite universe, and did so with an apocalyptic finality. Surely it is not accidental that Newton's is the most apocalyptically obsessed mind in the world of thinking, for his is the mind that most definitively and finally brought an end to the heaven of the ancient world. But the theoretical demonstrations of the *Principia* are anticipated imaginatively in *Paradise Lost*, for the negative energy of Milton's Satan is paralleled by the ubiquity of Newton's absolute space, a space which is the boundless and uniform *Sensorium* of God, and which is everywhere present only by constituting duration and space. Blake had no difficulty in naming Newton's God as Satan, but Newtonian space and Miltonic energy are equally consequences of modern revolution, and they parallel if they do not express those political revolutions which soon were to sweep away all the order and authority of the past. But such deep and ultimate political revolution is possible only on the basis of a radical and final negation of the transcendent world, an apocalyptic negation which appears in the very voice and face of Milton's Satan.

Chapter Five

PRAXIS
AND
APOCALYPSE

The Final Presence of History

Mythical and narrative forms which envision and enact a total or cosmic movement and finality of history first appear in ancient apocalyptic literature, and there they are invariably grounded in an apprehension of the near advent of an ultimate end or eschaton. That eschaton is the end of the world in the fullest apocalyptic literature, and the imminence of its coming is in exact accordance with the intensity of apocalyptic faith. Apocalyptic literature did not arise out of a void, and one of its sources was ancient historiography, both biblical and classical, both sacred and profane. That historiography itself had arisen out of something like an eschatological crisis, a crisis posing an ultimate challenge to a people or a nation, a challenge to the deepest identity of a people and even a challenge to its survival. Thus Old Testament historiography arose in response to the advent of monarchy in Israel, a monarchy which threatened to sweep away the distinctive faith and identity of Israel, and a monarchy which from the beginning had been violently opposed by the prophets. It was the Persian threat to the very survival of Greece which engendered the history of Herodotus, just as the beginning of the disintegration of the Greek polis not only launched but shaped the history of Thucydides, and the institution of the Roman Empire gave birth to Livy and Tacitus. Certainly the historical owl of Minerva flies only at night, a night embodying an end of a previous day of identity.

Thus it was the Enlightenment which gave birth to the modern historical consciousness, the advent of a new world which made possible a truly new understanding of the ancient world, and that understanding could actually know the ancient world only by realizing its end. This is historical revolution of the highest order, and it was only possible on the basis of the real negation of the ancient world which had previously occurred in Western history. That ancient world is itself known, and actually known, by a form and mode of consciousness which realized itself by negating and transcending its ground in the classical and biblical worlds. Hence the classical and biblical worlds now appear as distant worlds, as truly previous and former worlds, and it is precisely thereby that they are now known and apprehended. Only with the birth of the modern historical consciousness does the past fully appear as irreversibly and finally past, and it is only in that form that the past can become the object of modern historical knowledge. Thereby, however, the past gains a distinctiveness that it never had before, and for the first time historical events stand out in their own uniqueness, as the advent of a past which is irrevocably past releases and actualizes a whole new identity of history. That identity is itself irreversible in its ground, for no matter what revisions historical thinking will effect, historical thinking itself will disappear if the past ceases to appear and be real as an irrecoverable past.

There are only three great modern historical thinkers — Hegel, Marx, and Nietzsche — but their thinking brought modern revolution to its theoretical consummation. Pure historical thinking begins with Hegel and already comes to an end in Nietzsche, but in that brief period the full conceptual meaning of our history was established. Almost singlehandedly Hegel created the foundations of systematic and conceptual historical thinking, just as Nietzsche singlehandedly brought those foundations to an end, an end which has perhaps only been fully realized in our own time. But these foundations made possible the incredible riches of modern historical understanding, and even if most historians know no more of these foundations than do most scientists of the foundations of modern science, it is nevertheless true that historical thinking will wither away apart from the solidity of these foundations, as we no doubt are now discovering. When this occurs it is not just historical thinking which comes to an end, but rather a whole world which is truly recognizable as a human world that thereby ends, or, at least, it comes to an end for the individual subject of consciousness. This end was logically realized by Hegel, but only actually enacted by Kierkegaard and Marx, the one realizing the pure subjectivity and the other the pure objectivity of consciousness.

A purely interior subjectivity wholly externalizes or objectifies historical thinking, and does so to establish the individually existing subject, a subject which can realize itself only by negating all historical consciousness. That negation goes hand in hand with the parallel negation of its dialectical counterpart, the negation of the interiority and individuality of consciousness, a negation fully realized by Marx, and a negation making possible a truly new stage of the historical consciousness. Now historical events for the first time become manifest as being wholly exterior and objective, as their subjective ground is revealed as an ideological ground, and a ground which will come to an end when history is consummated in a universal consciousness or a universal humanity. If a Kierkegaardian subjectivity makes possible a purely individual consciousness, a Marxist objectivity makes possible an understanding and a consciousness which is itself a historical actor, and a primary historical actor, an actor which realizes the actuality of history by making its objective or real identity manifest. This cannot fully or truly occur until subjective identity is ended, for subjective identity now stands unveiled as a false identity or a false consciousness, an identity which is finally nothing more than a reflection of a class consciousness. The very individuality of subjective consciousness is a certain sign of its class base, and of its ruling class or nonproletarian base, for that individuality embodies an exploitative power which realizes its uniqueness only by dehumanizing and degrading its social source, a process of dehumanizing exploitation which is necessary and essential to the very establishment of a unique individual identity standing outside of a common social or human world.

The Hegelian labor of the negative becomes wholly objective in Marx, and this leads to a new objective history which for the first time makes manifest a fully objective or material ground as the originating source of history and consciousness, and a ground which is itself evolving through the actuality of historical praxis to an eschatological or apocalyptic goal. It is ironic but nonetheless understandable that dialectical materialism should be the most overtly apocalyptic form of modern thinking, for Marxism takes the finality and irreversibility of history with total seriousness and apprehends the very necessity of the historical process as a purely negative process, a process which not only negates the past to realize the future, but which continually negates itself to realize its own activity and life. If all truly modern history is Marxist insofar as it makes manifest a fully material or objective ground, it can only be Marxist insofar as it knows that ground as a forward-moving or evolving ground, and a ground which realizes itself in the deep structures or material foundations of history. Marxist thinking and Marxist historiography are inevitably dependent upon this eschatological even if material ground, for with its disappearance history here loses all meaning.

If modernity is the consequence of the triumph of a uniquely modern revolution in society and consciousness, then that triumph itself almost immediately passes into crisis, and does so not in its periphery, but in its center, in the innermost source of its life and power. Significantly enough, no great visual art accompanies the initial triumph of modernity, but a crisis almost immediately occurs after the initial breakthrough of Romantic literature, a crisis fully manifest in Wordsworth and Coleridge just as it is in Schiller and Goethe, and a crisis which achieves a definitive expression, at least for the German mind, in *Faust* II, but a crisis which is manifest to all in the late Beethoven. Simultaneously, the political failure on the continent after the French Revolution witnesses to the depth of this crisis, although the victories of

Napoleon did effect the final defeat of feudal and medieval Europe, even if this defeat was not complete until World War I. The enormous success of the industrial revolution, and of the social revolution which it released, have hidden the comprehensive power of this crisis, but it is surely manifest in nineteenth-century drama and fiction, just as it is in the virtual end of philosophy after the death of Hegel. Indeed, Hegel himself was persuaded that the highest expressions of art had become a thing of the past, and only of the past, as the inner bond had been loosened between subjectivity and objectivity, and objectivity could now triumph apart from any actual subjective or interior realization. Therein, of course, Hegel anticipated both Kierkegaard and Marx, and so likewise did he give some meaning to his own reactionary political turn away from his early and even mature, revolutionary liberalism.

But it is impossible to imagine that Hegel himself could have anticipated Nietzsche, even though Nietzsche may well be the most Hegelian of post-Hegelian thinkers, and is so surely in his understanding of consciousness, for here Nietzsche is more Hegelian than Hegel by understanding the totality of consciousness as the total negation of a pure negation, as the reverse embodiment of a pure and total negativity. That revolutionary conversion which issued in *Thus Spoke Zarathustra* went far beyond Nietzsche's initial Hegelian understanding of the death of God as the advent of modernity, and did so by historically realizing the death of God as both the beginning and the end of consciousness. Hegel's Calvary of absolute Spirit is the self-negation or the self-emptying of God, a self-emptying which is realized in the negative modes and movements of consciousness, and which is fully realized both historically and essentially in the total actualization of self-consciousness in the modern world. But Nietzsche's Zarathustra realizes self-consciousness itself as a total and totally self-constituting act, a *causa sui* which fully realizes and embodies itself in its own act, and in the power and the will of that very act. Then the Calvary of Spirit or the death of God is realized as the will to power, and therewith perishes every identity which stands outside itself, as the subject and the object of consciousness pass into a unity in which each ceases to be itself.

Zarathustra's animals celebrate that unity in their ecstatic vision of the dance and joy of Eternal Recurrence; now all identities and all events flow into one another, and they do so precisely by way of their most immediate actualization: "Being begins in every Now." And that actualization is a total actualization, an actualization in which everything whatsoever is totally present, and is present by way of the total release and embodiment of consciousness. Yet this very embodiment of consciousness is made possible by a historical realization of the origin and identity of consciousness. Only a full realization that the totality of consciousness is a historical consequence of the origin of the bad conscience can make possible a full reversal of consciousness in a total act of Yes-saying, an act and an affirmation transforming all identity whatsoever. Once consciousness is truly known as a consequence of the pure negativity of No-saying or the bad conscience, then both the center and the periphery of consciousness can be known as a pure negativity, and the reversal of that pure guilt or negativity issues in the full embodiment of consciousness, an embodiment in which consciousness becomes fully actual by ceasing to be or to will everything which is not fully and totally itself. The total reversal of consciousness then becomes manifest as the full realization of the death of God, and consciousness itself passes into full actuality by reversing its negative ground so as to realize that ground itself in a total presence, a pure immanence in which the totality of actual identity is totally present here and now.

THE LANGUAGE OF PRAXIS

It is common to date the advent of a fully modern language with the publication of Baudelaire's *The Flowers of Evil* in 1857. Just as the revolutionary poetic language of Homer preceded the revolutionary plastic language of Greek art, so, too, the full advent of modern poetry precedes the birth of modern art, and both occur long before their political counterparts, which are realized only in the twentieth century. Modern poetic language is a truly new language insofar as the subject and object of consciousness pass into each other in the actuality of language itself, and thereby language assumes and realizes a new identity of its own, an identity in which neither subject nor object stands forth only as itself. The "I" of the Romantic lyric then becomes inaudible and invisible as well, as a total presence becomes speakable which is the voice of world itself. No longer is that voice a uniquely individual voice, just as world is no longer apart and without. While this voice initially sounded in Romantic poetry, and therein achieved its primal integrity and power, it is only in and after Baudelaire that the true poetic voice ceases to be a unique and individual voice and becomes a voice transcending any possible individual ground or source.

Perhaps the most comprehensive realization of modern poetic language is in Joyce's *Ulysses*, where poetry passes into the prose of a world that is a concrete and historical day. Our historical actuality achieves an epiphany in *Ulysses*, and while this is a uniquely Joycean epiphany, its uniqueness lies not in the interior individuality of the artist, but rather in the fullness of a language that unites an exterior totality with a cosmos of interior and immediate centers. In his early and unfinished autobiographical novel, *Stephen Hero*, Joyce presented his initial vision of epiphany wherein even the commonest objects can leap out at us with a radiant presence when they present themselves as just what they are. But individual objects do not undergo an epiphany in *Ulysses*, or not as individual objects, for *Ulysses* is a fully historical cosmos in which objects are present only through subjects, and a human cosmos in which objects achieve their epiphany in the actuality of a fully human voice and consciousness. What is most unique about *Ulysses* is its enactment of a human cosmos which is totally and immediately present, and it is present at once both as world and as individual subject, but that subject is not an isolated and unique subject, but rather a universal and actual interiority wherein every center is only itself but is itself only insofar as it makes actual the presence of another. And not only the presence of another, but the presence of world itself, and a world which is itself only insofar as it is present and actual in language and consciousness.

Even at the time that *Ulysses* was being created, the Western world was in process of historical disintegration and each of the multiple foundations of Western culture and society passed through a series of cataclysmic shocks. That imminent chaos that again and again had been envisioned by nineteenth-century prophets, and above all by Kierkegaard, Marx, Nietzsche, and Dostoevski, fully burst forth in Europe, and simultaneously did so both in the political and the cultural realms, as an old world truly came to a comprehensive end. What had once been manifest as the individual human person soon vanished from history, or from its real expressions and life, and not only is this true in the birth of political totalitarianism, but also in the triumph of that new anonymous consciousness which occupies and soon dominates every expression and mode of life. The devils that Dostoevski had foreseen seemed to become incarnate in Soviet Russia and Nazi Germany, and a demonic fury was unleashed upon the world, a fury that has not yet abated. But it is in the death camps of Stalin and Hitler that this fury is most purely present, a fury not even remotely present in the past, for not only is the number of the victims of the death camps far larger than all the previous such victims in history, but never before has a political power given itself to the systematic and total degradation of its victim, as though only a human holocaust of monstrous proportions could sustain the existence of the State. The Western conscience crumbled before this holocaust, revealing that its roots had already withered away, for it is only in the twentieth century that a truly demonic horror becomes fully and actually embodied in history.

It is in the midst of this horror that the modern artist exercises his or her vocation, and we are not to wonder that so many art forms perished or were radically transformed during this period, for not one was left standing as it once was, and such a revolutionary transformation of the arts is integrally related to the social revolutions of the twentieth century. But just as twentieth-century art and literature have evolved out of nineteenth-century art and literature, so likewise have the social revolutions of the twentieth century evolved out of nineteenth-century political, social, and economic revolution. What is far more difficult to recognize is that the revolutionary power of twentieth-century art, literature, and music has a genuine parallel in the triumphant power of a twentieth-century social revolution, a revolution gradually but decisively bringing an end to the integral or intrinsic human identity and reality of every partial or even particular expression of consciousness. Initially, we can note the power of this revolution when we note that it is no longer possible poetically to speak of man, or humanity, or the human world, or even the human being. Nor can our painting or our sculpture now portray what was once manifest as a uniquely human identity and presence, just as our music has evolved a voice in which the human and the nonhuman are so conjoined as to preclude the possibility of the presence of a distinctively and uniquely human voice. But this dissolution of a unique interior identity in twentieth-century art is accompanied not only by an assault upon all individual identity in twentieth-century political totalitarianism but also by an erosion and erasure of the individual in modern technological and mass society.

This is a revolution so awesome that we have only begun to recognize and understand it; but it is clearly apparent that the language of this revolution is already present in Baudelaire, and that the evolution of modern poetry ever more comprehensively extends this revolution throughout the whole domain of consciousness and experience, as can be seen not only in Rimbaud and Mallarmé, but also in Hopkins, Yeats, Eliot, Pound, Stevens, and Williams, as poetic language itself negates and transcends every previously established human identity, and does so most forcefully and most finally in its most triumphant and fully realized expressions. If modern poetry has transcended Romantic poetry, it has done so most clearly in its negation and dissolution of an interior and individual consciousness; thereby a truly new poetic language has been spoken, and it has given us an exaltation going beyond a Keats or a Shelley. Perhaps this exaltation is spoken most ecstatically by the Rilke of *The Duino Elegies* and *The Sonnets to Orpheus*, and it is all too significant that the Heidegger of *Being and Time* who was inspired by Rilke could find no philosophical language to express this exaltation, and thereafter underwent a turn in which he altogether ceased speaking about an individual or interior consciousness. Even if it is true that all poetry transcends conceptual understanding, it is also true that a far greater chasm now stands between the poet and the philosopher than stood between Goethe and Hegel or Coleridge and Schelling, as both the darkness and the light of modern poetry stands beyond all systematic comprehension.

THE IDENTITY OF PRAXIS

While it is fully manifest that the demonic horror of the twentieth century resists and transcends all moral analysis, it should also be clear that our art and our literature likewise transcend all moral judgment, and do so with a finality that is not present in Western language and vision before Baudelaire. Nietzsche's realization that we are beyond good and evil was a prophetic response to historical reality, a reality that is manifest to all in the twentieth century, and a reality that is present in our triumphs just as fully as it is present in our defeats. Can it be accidental that the century which is witnessing the dissolution and reversal of self-consciousness is also witnessing the revolutionary advent of the masses? Ours may well be the most demonic of centuries, but it is also the century in which the great majority of humanity first found an actual and historically realizable voice and identity. Not until the twentieth century does a real assault upon world poverty and disease become an actual possibility, nor had it ever previously been possible for the majority to participate in any way in government or be given the possibility of any kind of formal education. None of these revolutionary transformations occurred before the interior disintegration of the West, just as none occurred before the beginning of the collapse of Western imperial power. If we may now justifiably speak of the advent of a world civilization, it is a civilization which is in process of transcending everything which was once manifest as the conscience and the consciousness of the West.

Perhaps every revolution releases its own demonism, and if the social and political revolutions of the twentieth century have generated a unique totalitarianism, it may well be that the very center of a genuine revolution can generate its own deepest and most violent reaction. Let us recall that something very like this happened with the origin of Christianity, and Christianity soon came to embody a political demonism of its own, a demonism grounded in absolute intolerance, a total religious intolerance that has never been seen either before or since in history. Of course, an absolute intolerance is present in totalitarianism, and perhaps we should identify it as a religious intolerance, but if so we should also recognize that it, too, is grounded in an initial and revolutionary reversal of consciousness. Both the Inquisitor and the Commisar are instruments of a totalitarian power promising total liberation, and each does so in the name of the transcendence of an old humanity, a humanity which is transcended by the very advent of true revolution or revelation. But totalitarian powers which are the embodiment of revolution can generate their own negation and transcendence, as witness those apocalyptic forces released by medieval Christendom which historically culminated in modern revolution.

Our moral categories cannot address our revolutionary history if only because those categories themselves are the product of a prerevolutionary history, or, rather, the product of the historical revolutions of Greece and Israel which are themselves transcended by modern revolution. What we have known as conscience and moral judgment is grounded in a fully individual conscience and consciousness, and with the collapse and transformation of that conscience and consciousness all which was once present as moral judgment becomes groundless. That groundlessness can be seen in the vacuity of our moral language, just as it can be seen in the inability of our moral judgment to confront the actualities of either culture or power, and worse yet in the almost invariable presence of a traditional moral language in the deepest expressions of social and political reaction. At this point in history it would appear that no moral thinker is any longer alive, or, at least, none who can have any impact upon our society, or upon any society within our historical horizon. Morally ours is the darkest of times, but nevertheless it is also that time and that unique historical time which continues to promise a revolutionary advance for the majority of humanity.

Is it possible to conjoin an understanding of the actual advent of a universal hand and face and voice with a realization of the actual disappearance of an interior center of self-consciousness? By this means we could realize that the negation and transcendence of an individual and interior self-consciousness goes hand in hand with the realization of a universal humanity, a humanity that can neither be named nor apprehended by an interior and individual voice. We might also thereby see that it is precisely the individual conscience and the individual consciousness that are the deepest obstacles to the realization of a universal humanity, a humanity that can be born only by a negation and transcendence of every previous historical configuration and voice of consciousness. It is the real negation of our own interior identity which opens us to a universal presence, a negation which is fully manifest in an Amos or a Paul, just as it is manifest in a parallel manner in Socrates and Confucius, each of whom could realize a new virtue or righteousness only by negating an old social or historical identity. That old reality was imbedded at the very center of that given reality which each of these prophets initially confronted, and while we know little or nothing about the individual consciousness of Amos, Socrates, and Confucius, we know that Paul could realize the identity of a new righteousness only by realizing an interior negation of that old Adam who is Saul of Tarsus. Apart from that negation, the new Adam would be unrealized and therefore unreal.

The social and political revolutions of the twentieth-century have either violently or silently assaulted all of the previously established identities of either the real or authentic human being, and have done so with such force as to engender an overwhelming reaction, a reaction which has either destroyed all civilization or stretched it to its very limits. But this reaction has not issued in the rebirth of a prerevolutionary center of consciousness, or, at least, none which has had an impact upon politics or the arts; instead it has been followed by an ever deeper erosion of premodern values and identities, with the result that these now have meaning only insofar as they are wholly distant from our midst. Consciousness itself can now appear in all its forms only as a broken and divided consciousness, and such a profound fissure of consciousness has succeeded in abolishing the intrinsic ground of every positive or normative identity. Thereby the intrinsic value or even meaning of any isolated form or mode of consciousness has been brought to an end, and brought to an end at the very points where a new and universal humanity appears and becomes real. It is now all too apparent that what we have known as the heights and depths of the individual and interior consciousness were inseparable from the silence and the impotence of the great bulk of humanity, and as that greater humanity begins decisively to speak and act, it does so in those empty voids or spaces created by the contraction of a former identity and voice.

Is it possible for us to affirm, and passionately to affirm, our own interior and individual dissolution as the way to the realization of our own full and universal humanity? But this way has already been established by our poets, and here poet and prophet are one just as prophet and poet are one, and one because the new and anonymous language which we have been given is a real and decisive way to the actual realization of a new humanity. No doubt a new humanity will appear to the individual consciousness as a new prison and a new grave, but now the only other humanity before us is a truly old humanity, and an old humanity which we all know to be dead or dying, for it has long since become impossible to celebrate or even to know its actual presence. Indeed, the celebration that we have known has issued from a passage through the end or death of an individual center of interiority, as most forcefully enacted by Nietzsche and Rilke, but enacted with a far more comprehensive power in Yeats and Stevens, and given an epic expression by Joyce. Perhaps only nothingness or a void can lie beyond such celebration, but apocalypticism has always known that the advent of the new world brings an end to the old, and we at least have been given glimpses of a new world in the very advent of a new and universal humanity. Our only question can be whether or not that humanity is our own.

Chapter Six

THE
SOLITUDE
OF
THE END

THE TIME OF THE END

The advent of a world civilization is the final realization of
both a comprehensive revolution in the modern West and the
disintegration of all premodern societies and cultures throughout the world. Just as Christendom has collapsed or been
wholly transformed in the West, the classical cultures of Asia
are perishing with an incredible rapidity, and it would appear that there is little hope of a real revival of the Islamic
world. The discipline of anthropology is a paradigm of our
situation, for even as it evolved to discover and comprehend a
vast new world of cultures and societies, its very apprehension
of this world went hand in hand with a dissolution and erasure of the object of its study. Our historical world and
understanding is far larger than it has ever been before, but it
is also far smaller, indeed, infinitely smaller, for history has
become a museum in our time, a graveyard of dead societies

and cultures. We have no Hölderlins who can now revive an ancient world, nor Hegels who can ground a present and contemporary understanding in an understanding of the past, nor Nietzsches who can employ an ancient symbolic language as a way into the present and the future. Whatever future can appear before us is a future wholly dissociated from the past, or wholly dissociated from everything which we can actually and historically know as the past. Knowledge itself is now the knowledge of death, the knowledge of that which is most removed from anything which is actually manifest to us as movement or life.

Nevertheless, even as the Christian must now look upon the collapse of the ancient world as the inevitable historical consequence of the birth of Christianity, so, too, the Christian must now look upon the collapse of our past as the way to an apocalyptic and eschatological future. Christianity, even as all religious ways, knows death as the way to life, and knows an actual passage through death as the way to an actual realization of life. Of course, this way is a universal way, and perhaps it is most powerfully present in ritual, and above all in that pure or archaic ritual which is uncontaminated by modernization, a ritual wherein resurrection is wholly illusory and unreal apart from its manifestation and realization as crucifixion. It is all too significant that at the very time when an ancient ritual was abandoned by the Church that an archaic ritual was reborn in our theater, our poetry, and our art and music, a rebirth that had already been definitively realized in *Finnegans Wake*, and also perhaps interiorly realized in orthodox psychoanalysis. Nothing so forcefully reveals the poverty of the Church today as the shallowness and superficiality of its ritual, a superficiality which is most manifest when ritual is most contemporary and updated, for it is precisely the contemporary world which is most distant from the archaic world, and even if a new sociology is revealing the ritual ground of our daily life, it does so only when it knows that life apart from any kind of historical identity.

Finnegans Wake may well be an awakening of the dead, but if so it is a consequence of the return of our history to a full ritual and mythical identity, and an identity which is realized only by way of an absolute reversal of our interior consciousness. The archaic world which is manifest in *Finnegans Wake*, however, is not susceptible to any kind of anthropological or historical understanding, just as the mythical world of this eschatological novel has no real point of contact with any past or historical mythology, but that is just the reason why *Finnegans Wake* remains a novel, even if the last possible novel, for it is an all too realistic and actual vision of an eschatological but historical reversal of our consciousness. This is the last story which can be told in our time, all our other stories are but faint or fragmentary retellings of this one, and if we know an end which is a beginning that is only because the only beginning which we can know is the beginning of the end. True, the innocent among us may be drawn to science fiction and other fantasies, but science fiction is neither science nor fiction, for fiction came to an end with that ultimate horror released by the death camps, and with the publication of *Finnegans Wake* in 1939. This was the very moment when America fully entered the world stage, only to be the victor of a war which finally brought our history to an end, as Captain Ahab stepped forth as the victor over the white whale.

Of course, Ahab remains lashed to the whale's back, just as

a triumphant America was bound to a dead body of history, thereby making possible not a resurrection of the dead, but rather a passage of death into the fullness of American society and culture. Now America stood forth as the first truly and fully modern nation, the very vanguard of a total modernization, and thus the exemplary model of a new world civilization. Apocalyptic believers might fancy America as the Antichrist, for it is closer to the end of history than a far more reactionary Soviet Union, and swarming with "poets" and "prophets" who claim to be the final spokesmen of the end. While Bosch's *The Ship of Fools* seems to have been reborn in America, far more than any such traditional identity is now at hand, for the end of history has already entered the public life of America, and perhaps most so in the very advent of a public life which is separated and dissociated from all private or interior identity. No doubt we may find an ancient historical precedent to this in that period which marked the transition from the Roman Republic to the Roman Empire, and that period did create the first real distinction between public and private identity. Yet Horace and Vergil could celebrate an identity that is simultaneously public and private, whereas our poetry has lost all contact with the public realm just as our society is wholly liberated and estranged from any kind of interior domain.

The full actualization of modernization effects an erosion of all sanctions for social institutions in all their variety, ranging from marriage and the family to education and the business corporation to judicial and political authority. Ever increasingly, as modernization proceeds, authority and legitimacy in all their forms become totally objectified or fully exterior and external, thereby they are wholly divorced from internal assent or meaning, and therby they also wholly transcend all symbolic or imaginable identity. Objectification now realizes itself as a total presence throughout the whole domain of our public consciousness and life, an objectification, which Kierkegaard was the first to realize, is finally identical with the public realm. But as Kierkegaard so clearly and so prophetically foresaw, the dominance of a public and objective consciousness is only possible by way of the negation and dissolution of an individual and subjective consciousness. It was only left for a posthistorical America to demonstrate that religion, culture, and the arts can continue to be present and manifest even in the absence of an interior and individual consciousness. Indeed, even the most intimate subjective identities, and above all "love," can seemingly continue to exist apart from the presence of individuals, for "love" can now be present without individual enactment or participation. So, likewise, "faith" can apparently continue to be present, and even to present itself as being realized through individual decision, but that decision is at bottom an exterior or public act which can occur only by way of the absence of all interior individual enactment.

We do not need the imagery of "black holes" or thermonuclear explosion to envision an apocalyptic end, we only have to acknowledge the advent of a totally alien and totally present objectivity, an objectivity which brings a real and historical end to all actual or individual subjectivity, and does so with a total and irreversible finality. The actuality of our history is now realizing such an objectivity, and whether or not it will triumph with an irreversible finality, it already is true that even those pockets of our history which hide an all too fragmentary individual presence are rapidly receding into our past, and it is no longer possible even to record their diminishing presence, as real fiction has virtually vanished and poetry has all but lost the possibility of speaking in an individual voice. But most revealing of all, it is not possible for us either to envision or to name a totally present objectivity. Yes, we know it as an anonymous presence, can envision it as a vacuous presence, and perhaps can hear it as a tonally atonal presence. But we cannot truly name or fully envision that presence if only because its actual totality transcends all vision and all naming, and, indeed, as its totality becomes ever more fully manifest its very presence stills and dissolves the possibility of speech and vision, and does so at the very center of vision and speech.

THE WAY OF THE END

Our interior center is passing ever more fully and more finally into an exterior actuality, and this occurs not only in the public realm of society but also in the interior domain of intimate encounter, as a universal or total humanity is dawning which negates and transcends every interior and historical identity. But how is it possible to speak of a new universal humanity if its dawning totality is erasing all established historical and social identities? Silence is now ever more fully manifest as the new voice of speech, and this is not a silence which is confined to a purely objective presence, but also a silence which occurs in the innermost voice of speech. Such a silence realizes and embodies both an exterior and an interior negativity, a pure negativity which releases itself by reversing all given or established identity, and does so most forcefully and most finally at the center of identity and voice. A kenotic

or self-emptying center is now passing into a full and final actuality, and as that actuality realizes itself in our midst, a
pure negativity becomes both our innermost and our outer-
most identity, a total identity and a total presence which even
now is becoming all in all.

Silence has always been the deepest language of ritual, just
as it has been the purest language of the classical mystical
ways. But the silence enacted in archaic ritual and interior
mystical vision precludes the possibility of historical enactment, and does so because a ritual or a purely mystical silence
inactivates all movement and process and disengages all pas-
sion and will. Whereas ritual and mystical silence still and
dissolve all given identity, the historical actualization and
embodiment of silence reverses and transforms a socially and
historically established identity, thereby releasing the actuality of silence in the domain of common and public reality.
Now silence is enacted throughout the vicissitudes of life, and
enacted and embodied wherever an interior identity presents
itself, thereby effecting a comprehensive negation and reversal of every interior and individual presence. It is human
identities in all their richness which are now collapsing, and
whether these be those of nation and work, or sex and race, or
marriage and the family, all sanctions for these and all such
social identities are coming to an end, and coming to an end
at just those points where these identities are most actual and
real, as the grounds for every social and historical particularity are dissolving in our midst.

One by one our innermost identities are perishing in their
actuality, and this occurs precisely in our deepest and purest
acts of will, in those acts and moments when energy and life
are most fully present, and we are most truly ourselves. Such

moments are simultaneously an interior and an exterior actuality, and they occur simultaneously as interior and historical or objective acts, as acts which are both our own and
another's, and are our own only insofar as their origin wholly
lies outside us. Therein every fixed or given identity perishes
within us, but that perishing is realized in act, in an act which
is intimately and interiorly our own only by way of being realized beyond us, and wholly beyond us in an actuality which is
free of every sign or mark of our individual presence. It is just
this process, and the fullness and finality of this process,
which negates and reverses every particular face or mask of
consciousness, as every unique and individual face now passes into a negative and anonymous mask, and face as face is
real only insofar as it is negatively present as mask. Thus a
No-drama is being enacted among us, and enacted by way of
the gestures and movements of our masks, but that drama is
actual and real only insofar as it enacts and embodies a total
and historical destiny, and a destiny which is realized in every
actual and actually individual presence.

No-dramas are very short and virtually plotless, just as are
the real moments of our lives, and they enact an archaic
presence, a presence which our lives know and realize as a
faceless anonymity. But that anonymity is inseparably related to the birth of a new humanity, a humanity which can be
realized only at the end of history, and only by way of a negation of all integral and intrinsic individuality or particularity.
That unique individuality which transcends the universal, an
individuality known by Kierkegaard and a host of modern
writers, transcends only the abstract or general universal, not
the concrete or actual universal which is present in the
historical advent of a truly new humanity. Now the true indi-

vidual is identical with the concrete or actual universal, but is so only by way of the negation of the particular, and above all the negation of that very particularity which is most interiorly present and near at hand. This negation occurs to realize the universal, to realize the concrete and actual universal, a universal which is present and real wherever individual identity now appears or stands forth. Yet the actual and concrete universal can never be envisioned or named as such by individual consciousness, or, rather, not named or envisioned in its actual totality, except insofar as that totality is negatively present and at hand.

Already in the proclamation of Jesus, a total presence realizes and presents itself only by way of its negative assault upon all given or established identity, and it is the reversal of the center or ground of established identity which actualizes a total and final presence. That final presence can only have a negative identity to any integral or individual form of consciousness, therefore it will be wholly manifest to that consciousness as judgment, and as a total judgment which consumes all given and individual identity. Once again such judgment is manifest among us, although never before has it been either so violent or so comprehensive as it has been in the twentieth century, nor has it ever previously truly or fully entered a public and objective history. Just as the horrors of the twentieth century are without real historical precedent, so likewise a total objectification or externalization of consciousness has never previously occurred, nor have language and the imagination ever before been so immediately and so totally embodied by a pure negativity. That negativity is now present in all our language and all our acts, or is so present when we ourselves are actually and immediately present, which is to say in those moments and acts in which we are most alive and real. Those are the moments wherein we enact a pure negativity, wherein self-judgment, and total self-judgment, becomes immediately actual, but it is the actuality of such pure judgment which reverses all given identities of consciousness, thereby making possible the actual realization of a new and universal humanity.

Therefore it is possible to understand the actuality of pure judgment as grace, and as a pure and total grace which is everywhere, but it is everywhere only by being nowhere in individual and interior consciousness and experience. For an interior and individual presence of grace solidifies and sanctions an individual and interior identity, thereby making that identity more real to itself, and more real to itself as a subjective identity. Thus it is the very disappearance of grace in all individual interiority which makes possible its full objective realization. Pure subjectivity has progressively disappeared or been reversed in our history, and it is precisely the moments of such subjective disappearance and reversal that are the only moments which we have actually known and named as grace. These are the moments when speech and vision have most fully been given us, and they are also the moments when a universal hand and face have been present and actual in consciousness, a face and hand that can only appear and act through the disappearance of all unique and particular identity. It is just the disintegration of all unique interior identity which makes possible the actual realization of a concrete universality, a concrete universality which is historically enacted and embodied, and embodied by way of the negation and reversal of all individual interiority.

The end of history is the end of a unique and individual

consciousness, and even if it was only by way of this consciousness that a full historical consciousness came into existence, it is also true that it is just the reversal of a unique interiority that embodies a universal consciousness. As opposed to a mystical universal consciousness which is totally passive and inactive, an embodied universal consciousness is present in objective and historical acts, in acts which are present in the fullness of history, even if the fulfillment of these acts brings history to an end. That end has already dawned in the disintegration of a pure interiority, and as that disintegration is enacted again and again throughout the fullest moments of our lives, a concrete universality is actually embodied among us, and even if it is impossible for an individual voice or consciousness to name or envision that universality, it nevertheless is true that we know that universality to be real, and know it to be real because it is realized among us, and realized among us in the deepest and most actual moments of our own interior disintegration. For those are the moments when we are given another, another who is most distant from ourselves, and above all most distant from a unique and individual "I." Such an "I" is infinitely distant from an embodied presence, and so much so that only a reversal of that "I" can truly embody presence. But the embodiment of that presence makes possible the embodiment of a universal presence, and therefore the actual historical realization of a universal consciousness.

ABSOLUTE SOLITUDE

On December 26, 1910, Kafka remarked in his journal that being alone had a power over him that never fails: "My interior dissolves (for the time being only superficially) and is ready to release what lies deeper." But how is it possible to be alone in the twentieth century? A better question would be: Has there ever before been a time when solitude is the very condition of individual existence? Historically, actual solitude was born in the eighth century B.C.E. in Greece and Israel, and it was accompanied by a parallel birth at something like this time in India. This was a unique historical moment when an individual form of consciousness broke through the previous collective or corporate identity of consciousness, and did so in such a way as to make possible a truly individual act and enactment of consciousness. But ours is the time of the end of a unique and individual consciousness, and the end of that consciousness is the end of history as well, and the beginning of a posthistorical time when an integral and interior individuality will have disappeared. Yet how is it possible to move beyond the dissolution of the interior to what lies deeper?

Initially, it would appear that the depths of solitude lie in schizophrenia, for we fantasize these depths as a fully literal solitude, a solitude removed from all real contact with anything outside itself. But it is possible to imagine an opposite solitude. Just as the Upanishads could know a cosmic and universal Atman lying beneath the depths of all conscious individuality, so modern abstract painting has envisioned a totality lying deeper than any individual identity, and modern poetry has given us concrete images of a pure immediacy which is beyond all individual and interior presence. Common sense and common language might judge all of these visions to be schizophrenic, but all of us know better, and we know better because we know in some indubitable sense that these visions are real. Moreover, these visions are of world-historical significance; the Upanishads gave birth to the higher civilization of India, which later became the ground of a universal Buddhism, and modern art and poetry are the historical consummation of the revolutionary consciousness of the West. And that consciousness is political as well as imaginative, indeed, is most political when it is most imaginative, even if the apparent inheritors of revolution in the twentieth century are the most violent enemies of modern art. Those are the enemies who are most dedicated to the violent destruction of all interior consciousness, and the power of their dedication can tell us something of the reality of those visions which they so forcefully oppose.

It is also beyond our own interiors that we discover the reality of the insulted and the oppressed. Now it is a matter of overwhelming significance that the insulted and the oppressed were not discovered in the ancient world, neither in the East nor in the West; that discovery does not truly occur until St. Francis, and then it goes underground in the West only to burst forth violently in the nineteenth century. True, the voices of the insulted and oppressed speak passionately in the English Revolution, nor are they silent in the French Revolution even if they had been in the American Revolution, but it is not until Marx that these voices fully affect history. If Marxism is the fullest or at least the most open embodiment of the oppressed masses of humanity, it is a matter of grave note that it is precisely here that one can discover the fullest negation of an interior individuality, a negation without which there could be no dialectical materialism. Here, the actual depths of humanity only appear by way of the dissolution of the interior, for it is only by way of that dissolution that the masses can stand forth as the true actors of history. Even if there is a negation of this negation in Marxist-Leninism, a negation reenacting the Church's negation of Jesus, it remains all too true that it is not since Dostoevski that the insulted and the oppressed have spoken and been present in an individual and interior moment and mode of consciousness.

Only by going beyond our own interior can we reach those deep crevices leading to a truly common and universal humanity. It is an illusion, and a demonic and perverse illusion, that a common humanity is simply that humanity which seems to be at hand, or which is most visible or most audible in a mass culture and a mass society. A common humanity is just what is most invisible and inaudible in our society, for the mass humanity that is audible and visible to us is the opposite of a common humanity, and opposite because it is a wholly artificial and unreal humanity, an electronic humanity as played by the "organ stop" of Dostoevski's underground man. Only an underground consciousness can now know humanity, and that means a solitary consciousness, a consciousness existing beyond ours or any interiority. But is it not true that none of us can now discover a human presence except in those rare moments when we are delivered from our own interiority, and delivered not by physical intoxication or cultural drugs, but rather by the actual presence of another, another who can never appear within, and never appear by way of anything which is a truly individual voice or gesture? The one so present is certainly not a person or a self, being neither male nor female, neither old nor young, neither black nor white. Self-consciousness is just what is most missing from all which we can know as a truly human presence, and the very absence of self-consciousness in our deepest and most actual moments is a decisive sign of the identity of that common humanity which has dawned in our time. True solitude is the opposite of pure ego, and the opposite because self-consciousness is absent in deep solitude, a truth which is fully manifest in the plenary moments both of our literature and of our art. Genuine solitude can never be chosen or even willed, it comes when we least expect it, and it comes to deliver us from everything which is only our own. Perhaps music most immediately calls us to such solitude, and when we genuinely listen to music we never listen with our own ears, which is to say that we do not and cannot then listen with ears which are only our own, which hear only our own silence and speech. One of the greatest gifts of our technological age is that it is now possible for the first time for each of us to listen to music alone, so that now we can listen to music with the depth with which we read; nor is it to be forgotten that neither the printed book nor silent reading came into existence until the close of medieval Europe, which is yet another clear mark of the uniqueness of modern history. For even if our history has ushered in a full objectification of consciousness, it has also given us profoundly solitary moments, and deeply solitary modes of existence and life.

Manuals of meditation in East and West call for a deep and profound movement within, but that is not a movement deeper into ego or self-consciousness, it is rather a movement which leaves self-consciousness and ego behind. Now, even if an actual self-consciousness is absent from the ancient world, it is nevertheless true that selfhood and ego are present, and present as the deepest foils and obstacles to the religious way.

For even the individual faith for which the Old Testament prophets called demanded a radical movement outside of all the given identities of a social and corporate selfhood. All of these ancient religious movements are movements into solitude, and they realize and enact themselves by way of solitude, for it is precisely the most total moments of solitude which make manifest and real a total presence of the holy or the divine. Apparently all such solitude has vanished from our history, but a radical solitude has been present with us nonetheless, and this solitude is opening us to a total and comprehensive vision. That vision is partially released in our actual moments of genuine solitude, and then a new humanity is present, a humanity which we can neither conceive nor define. But we know it to be a new humanity, for it is given to us as a new humanity, a universal humanity which is wholly beyond any identity which can interiorly be present, and beyond every interior and individual identity which we can know. Nevertheless, in moments of genuine solitude we know such a humanity to be present, and we know it to be present because it is in just such moments that our identities pass beyond an interior realm and realize a depth wherein everything which is present is not our own.

Genuine solitude is a voyage into the interior, but it is a voyage which culminates in a loss of our interior, a loss reversing every manifest or established center of our interior so as to make possible the advent of a wholly new but totally immediate world. The joy of solitude comes only out of a breakthrough releasing us from our own interior, a breakthrough and a joy which is clearly present when we fully listen to music, and it is no less present in the presence of another, but only when that other has no point of contact with our own within. Then the voice and the gesture of another are in no sense our own, and it is just for that reason that they are immediately present, and immediately present in the domain of what had just been own own interior. For that interior is not truly or actually our own, and thus genuine solitude releases us from the power of our own interior, and in such moments we know and fully know that every interior which is our own has actually come to an end. But the real end or reversal of an individual interior makes possible the actual advent of a universal presence, a presence transcending all interior and individual identity, and presenting itself beyond our interior, and beyond every possible interior, as a total and immediate presence.

Perhaps nowhere is the immediacy of a total presence more manifestly present than in the fullest moments of American jazz, and it is significant that jazz is the only art which is the consequence of a fusion between an archaic spirit and modern art, just as it is the only art which is a consequence of the coincidence of two racial worlds. No interior is present when jazz is most fully released, for the voice of the blues which made possible this release is a purely negative voice, a voice whose very purity is directed against the interiority of voice. The power embodied in jazz violently shatters our interior, as its pure rhythm both returns us to an archaic identity and hurls us into a new and posthistoric universality. Most startling of all, the "noise" of jazz releases a new silence, a silence marked by the absence of every center of selfhood, the disappearance of the solitude of the "I." That silence is the silence of a new solitude, an absolute solitude which has finally negated and reversed every unique and interior ground of consciousness, thereby releasing the totality of consciousness in a total and immediate presence. And we rejoice when confronted with this solitude, just as we rejoice in hearing jazz, for the only true joy is the joy of loss, the joy of having been wholly lost and thereby wholly found again. Not only is the only true paradise the paradise that we have lost, but the only regained paradise is the final loss of paradise itself.